IT'S NOT ALWAYS RIGHT TO BE RIGHT

IT'S NOT ALWAYS RIGHT TO BE RIGHT

AND OTHER HARD-WON LEADERSHIP Lessons

HAMISH THOMSON

WILEY

First published in 2021 by John Wiley & Sons Australia, Ltd

42 McDougall St, Milton Qld 4064
Office also in Melbourne

Typeset in Utopia Std 10.5pt/14pt

ISBN: 978-0-730-38907-1

A catalogue record for this book is available from the National Library of Australia

Cover design by Paul McCarthy / Wiley

Chapter opener image credits: chapter 3: Scott Olson/Getty Images; chapter 4: Allstar Picture Library Ltd / Alamy Stock Photo; chapter 5: AF archive / Alamy Stock Photo; chapter 6: PA Images / Alamy Stock Photo; chapter 8: jeremy sutton-hibbert / Alamy Stock Photo; chapter 9: Jeff Morgan 13 / Alamy Stock Photo; chapter 10: dpa picture alliance / Alamy Stock Photo; chapter 11: AAP/ AP Photo / Alan Welner; chapter 12: BRIAN HARRIS / Alamy Stock Photo; chapter 13: Image reproduced from *Teiho Kenzeiki Zue* (訂補建撕記図会 乾) by Kenzei. chapter 14: ZUMA Press, Inc. / Alamy Stock Photo; chapter 15: Pictorial Press Ltd / Alamy Stock Photo; chapter 18: PCN Photography / Alamy Stock Photo; close: Royal Geographical Society / Getty Images.

Disclaimer
The material in this publication is of the nature of general comment only, and does not represent professional advice. It is not intended to provide specific guidance for particular circumstances and it should not be relied on as the basis for any decision to take action or not take action on any matter which it covers. Readers should obtain professional advice where appropriate, before making any such decision. To the maximum extent permitted by law, the author and publisher disclaim all responsibility and liability to any person, arising directly or indirectly from any person taking or not taking action based on the information in this publication.

CONTENTS

Purpose

What's in it for You?

Over the years, I have regularly been asked to provide 'insights' and supposed 'wisdom' to others about the invaluable lessons that I have acquired throughout my career as a multinational CEO spanning continents, markets and industry segments.

In many ways, I cannot help but feel slightly embarrassed each time I'm asked for these stories. Whether this self-consciousness comes from my own humility or the ever-present imposter syndrome that we all seem to suffer from, I remain unsure.

One thing I do know is that I always seem to get positive feedback when I share these stories. From new recruits, eager graduates and hungry apprentices to seasoned executives and senior leaders, from dedicated factory folk to driven agency partners, anyone who cares to listen seems to get something out of it.

I know it sounds like a cliché, but 'if I knew then what I know now' I would have been so much better: more capable, more confident, potentially more successful and, most importantly, infinitely happier. So that's why I've written this book.

Will you walk away a completely different person after reading these pages? I very much doubt it.

But let's face it: life is damn hard at the best of times, particularly in the cut and thrust of the corporate world. Whether you're just starting out or you're a battle-hardened global leader, the demands of business are relentless.

So if you walk away from this book with one or two things that resonate strongly, go on to claim them as your own, and even stamp your leadership style on them, then hey, mission accomplished. If my insights help you to be just that much more self-assured and self-equipped for business success, then surely it's a good thing. Enjoy.

Best, Hamish

Introduction

Good, but not Great

Well, how does one start off a book when that particular someone has seldom passed chapter 3 of the thousand leadership books he's started reading over the years? With a degree of difficulty, I'd say. Let's go.

Before we start, let's be clear on a few things.

Firstly, I reckon I am good, but not great. I have been successful in the corporate world, yet I believe success is relative. I have worked in many different roles, functions, companies and geographies, yet I am no NYSE Top 10 CEO. I have reasonable intelligence and have been told I am strategic, and I have successfully motivated teams across all levels of an organisation.

I also have an insatiable drive for results. Sometimes too much drive, but we'll talk about that later. Above all, though, I love new. New ideas, new concepts, new ways of working. Anything that is different and anything that forces me out of my comfort zone. This works for some people, and it drives others crazy.

I cannot stand books (or people, for that matter) that talk endlessly about what we *should* do. Why we need to do this and why we must do that. Ones that list the reasons why we need to change, the problems we face, the struggles we encounter and the dilemmas in front of us — essentially, a hundred-plus reasons as to why we need to change — yet give no plan for action.

It drives me crazy. I am not against creating a compelling reason or vision for change, as that stuff is critically important as a catalyst for true change. I'm just against endless talk and bugger-all action.

How many times have you opened a management or leadership book that promises you the world, yet 100 pages into it you still haven't got one clue as to what you should do next? Nothing tangible, no clear insight and no concrete action plans to make a true difference.

Add to this the number of times you've been in presentations or meetings where clever people state clever facts, analyse complex issues, share passionate pleas about the world of pain your organisation is in and the need to act with immediacy and utter conviction, only to fail to provide any way forward.

I do not need (nor will I accept) an extended business version of *War and Peace* just saying what we already know. I just want the relevant facts followed by a clear and logical recommendation on what we should do next. Then let's just get on with it. Simple.

Now, back to the reason for the book itself. Unquestionably, I am better at business and a better leader today than I was when I was 20. Infinitely. (Some might say this was not a hard thing to achieve.)

I also know (like anyone who has worked on their self-awareness) that I have made numerous mistakes along the way. But mistakes give insight, and insight gives learning. This invaluable learning has shaped the success of not only myself, but of those around me and the brands and organisations of which I have been a part.

On the evening after I resigned from my position as Regional President of Mars Incorporated, I sat at the kitchen bench with a bottle of New Zealand pinot and proceeded to write down the key experiences, insights and learnings that I felt had shaped me over the last 30 years of my working life. Not technical or functional competencies, but true personal insights as a leader of others and as a leader of myself. By the time I had finished the bottle (and, rest assured, I am not a slow drinker) I had listed 67.

I can hear you sigh already, but you can relax: I won't bore you to death with all of them. Rather, just a key selection that I believe will provide some benefit to others. I don't expect to make my fortune from this, nor will I make any international bestseller list, but I do sincerely hope it makes a positive difference to those who read it. (And if it's just my three kids who do so, well, that will be success in my mind.)

Oh yes, one other important thing before we jump in. Close friends have asked me on numerous occasions why I even attempted writing this book. It's definitely a valid question and I reckon there are lessons in the answer for all of us.

The first reason is that I believe we should consistently push ourselves out of our comfort zone and I want this to resonate with all others. As I advise my partner, kids, colleagues and teams, just have a go and back yourself. You have nothing to lose. TS Elliot coined it beautifully when he wrote, 'If you aren't in over your head, how do you know how tall you are?' Personally, I always want to know how tall I can be.

And the second reason is that I am a massive believer in unlocking potential in others. As I have discovered over many a year, it only takes one new insight of significance to make a massive difference to your career — indeed, to your life. Unleashing this potential in others is one very cool feeling.

Those are the reasons.

A DISCLAIMER

Although I detest disclaimers (nowadays they appear at the base of virtually everything that you see, hear or read), here comes one: if you don't agree with some of my concepts, principles or supposed insights, that's okay. As you will soon see, I view most approaches in life as neither right nor wrong, just different. The concepts explored here work for me, and on the majority of occasions that I have shared them with others, they work for them too. That said, if they aren't for you, use them as provocation, stay curious and keep reading. If you disagree with *all* of them, simply look at chapter 8, 'Bad bosses are great bosses', change the word 'boss' to 'author', and all will be forgiven.

You will also observe that I have included a critique from a contributing author at the end of each chapter. Each is a respected expert within their field. I greatly value their opinions and believe their contributions, critques and reviews will be invaluable for you. I have provided them complete freedom to challenge, dispute, discard or build upon and support my positions. As you will discover, I love diverse perspectives, and these subject matter experts provide that.

As you progress through this book, you will also see that I have thrown in some practical strategic models. They are incredibly simple, which is why I like them and the reason that they work. People are often told in performance reviews, development discussions or general coaching sessions, 'I would like you to show more strategic agility'. This innocent, oft-used line can also be destructive and make people doubt themselves.

I believe that anyone with a reasonable level of intelligence has the ability to be strategic. Everyone can just step back, reflect a little, look at the broadest possible view first and then work backwards towards a solution. And if that fails, you can rattle off a few strategic models every now and then to show how clever you really are. Do this and you're halfway to becoming a strategic consultant.

There are literally thousands of these models out there, so please feel free to borrow, steal or beg from wherever takes your fancy. Claim them as your own, use them as your own, and, most importantly, lose the story that you are not strategic. It is unnecessary baggage that helps no-one.

Chapter 1

Law, Logic and Relationships

Quite an intense yet mischievous-looking chap, Ivan Petrovich Pavlov.

He was a Russian physiologist best known for his work in the 1890s in the field of classical conditioning. His well-known Pavlovian Theory involves pairing a stimulus with a conditioned response.

Relationships revolve around a similar concept: authenticity, vulnerability and transparency lead to levels of trust and partnership that in turn lead to breakthrough and transformation.

One is not possible without the other.

As Pavlov said, 'Perfect as the wing of a bird may be, it will never enable the bird to fly if unsupported by the air.'

Without effective relationships, growth—and, indeed, flight—is not achievable.

THE MESSAGE ·······················

Despite the thousands of hours that we spend trying to master technical and functional skills, they matter little unless you can truly develop the art of relationship building. We all know this; leaders, managers and colleagues talk about it regularly, and we see daily success from those who are good at it. Despite this knowledge, however, we do bugger-all about it. Hardly anyone in corporate life really knows how to focus on it, and, concerningly, even fewer know how to get better at it. Instead we consistently see brilliant individuals, whose ideas, innovations and creativity are phenomenal, fall at the very first hurdle. Conversely, I also feel sorry for people who are excellent at fostering relationships: seldom do they get recognised, rewarded or leveraged to the degree they deserve.

Law and logic are wonderful things. Invaluable. Very seldom, however, are they as important as relationships. Start with believing and knowing the importance of relationships. Then make and take the time to work on this skill set. Do not treat it as a 'nice to have', but rather a 'must do'. Track your progress and replicate. It will be transformational to your personal development and career, and it will also be your best chance of sustained success.

Above all, please do not just nod in agreement and then do nothing — that would be a waste.

···

Back in 2000, when I was first approached to join Mars Incorporated, I truly came to understand the adage 'don't judge a book by its cover'. First impressions are always important — in business and in life — yet often they obscure the true face that lies behind them.

We had recently returned to Australia from the Netherlands, had a new addition to the family — Dutch-born Harry — and we were champing at the bit for the next exciting chapter.

Following a brief stint in Melbourne, I got a call from a recruiter asking if I would be interested in joining the world of fast-moving consumer goods (FMCG or, as known in the United States, consumer packaged goods or CPG). To be honest, packaged goods had never really interested me up to that point. I had dealt with a few players in my London advertising days — Reckitt Benckiser, the home of Dettol, being the main one — and at the time, I remember naively thinking that it sounded a little boring.

Mars had generously arranged for us to visit them over a long weekend in the middle of June. The head office for their billion-dollar regional Petcare division was located in the twin city of Albury–Wodonga, right on the state border of New South Wales and Victoria. (Interesting fact: regardless of which side of the border you were born in Albury–Wodonga, you can change your state of birth as stamped in your passport to your preference. I was told this law was made for those born in Wodonga Hospital, where cricket- and footy-loving parents from New South Wales could not stand the thought of their kids growing up supporting Victoria. Considering the lengths to which I have gone in ensuring my kids emphatically support my beloved New Zealand All Blacks, this makes perfect sense.)

My wife Maddie and I still laugh about this initial visit. Having recently arrived in Australia, we had never heard of Albury, let alone Wodonga, and were still coming to grips with the fact that Mars not only made chocolate but also Pedigree. Either way, it turned out to be the trip from hell, and one that even the Griswolds would be proud of.

We are used to rain; lots of rain. We've lived in North West England, which is notorious for rain, and Amsterdam, which is no Maldives, and our early years of growing up in New Zealand certainly do not evoke memories of tropical sunshine. This, however, was something different. From the second we arrived to the minute we left, we suffered through torrential flooding and possibly one of the biggest storms we have ever experienced. The hotel where we stayed, Albury's biggest and brightest, was deserted. Apart from the dude at reception who had a mullet haircut that only his mother could love (I can get away with saying this, as I had one for most of my teenage years), there was no-one in sight.

Our hotel room was leaking — there were literally puddles of rainwater on the floor. Harry had a raging ear infection. Poor little kid, but I think we were calling him different names that weekend. Trying to save my marriage (Maddie was not exactly the happiest of campers at that stage), I ventured out to get as much alcohol as possible and rescue the situation with a takeaway. Unfortunately, my cheapskate mindset (yep, some Scottish blood in there) led me to the local Chinese restaurant, which ended up providing us with one of the dodgiest meals we have ever encountered. (To be fair, they probably weren't expecting anyone to be mad enough to venture out that night, but this dinner was dodgy, even by my lax standards.)

After a romantic evening, the next morning we were met by a real estate agent to show us around the area for possible future accommodation. Considering we could not see three feet in front of us, everything just looked shitty.

By the time I got into the office on Monday morning, I was faced with a day of passionate, full-on and energetic interviewing.

When you first entered those original Mars offices, you got one hell of a surprise. In this case, an unbelievably massive office space. It was almost the length of two rugby pitches joined together, with no partitions whatsoever. No filing cabinets to be seen. It was totally open plan, with clean-as-clean desks, bugger-all meeting rooms, and, where they did exist, they were all glass. Totally see through. What's more, the majority of them appeared to have no doors on them. What immediately struck me was the palpable energy pulsating throughout the space. No obvious divisions, hierarchies or bureaucracy. Just a totally transparent, collaborative way of doing business that I immediately warmed to.

Aside

While most companies went open plan in the 2000s, Mars has lived by this mantra virtually since its inception. Their no-fuss, totally egalitarian approach to office layout (which has created some sensational office spaces over the years), alongside their purpose-led family values, was game changing.

I should mention that prior to leaving the hotel that morning — Maddie still in pissed-off mode and Harry still crying — I tried to placate Maddie with the following peace offering: 'Oh well, darling, it was a free weekend, we got to see a new part of the country, and, rest assured, if I do end up being offered the role, relax: I'll just say thanks, but a very emphatic no thanks'.

You can guess what happens next.

Late in the day after the standard meet and greet interview process with what seemed like every man and his dog — excuse the pun — the Human Resources director pulled me into one of the infamous doorless offices. Before I could utter a word, he proceeded with something along the lines of, 'Hamish, the team really enjoyed the interactions today, we think you would be a great fit within the Mars family and we would like to offer you the role'. No mucking around. And with that, he passed over a half-opened envelope containing a letter of offer. After a quick glance, in which I noticed the salary figure in bold at the top of the sheet, I quickly replied, 'Yep, I think we can do this, Geoff!'

Without doubt, when you have a young family and only a vinyl record player to your name, money talks. Like many multinationals, Mars pay exceptionally well to attract the right talent to their regional locations.

Back to the not judging a book by its cover, Albury–Wodonga truly overcame its woeful first impression. We ended up having some of the happiest and most fulfilling times of our lives there. The area is sensational for raising a young family surrounded by people who would become lifelong friends; it is definitely hard to beat. The relationships we formed there have become central to our lives and, as you will shortly discover, relationships are the cornerstone to true business success. My apologies to the locals and definitely to the hotel reception dude — a.k.a. mullet boy — for my initial impressions. I was considerably wrong.

A LESSON I NEVER FORGOT

Now, this brings me to another thing that jumped out at me during that initial visit: law, logic and relationships.

During the interview process, I sat down with the head of Research & Development. Mars Petcare has one of, if not the, largest groups of food technologists in the southern hemisphere. It is truly amazing what thought leadership and expertise goes into looking after those little companion animals of ours.

Peter was one of those intellectual, science-background types who had enormous passion and drive in all that he did. I quickly came to admire him and loved his tenacity and constant search for continuous improvement. A lot of people talk it; he lived it.

I can't recall too much about our initial meeting apart from his very first question: 'So, Hamish, you were raised in New Zealand, lived most of your working life in Europe and have frequented the US on numerous occasions. In what order would you rank the importance of law, logic and relationships within each of these regions?'

Bloody hell. That took me by surprise. But I'm generally quite good on my feet and, employing the standard response that every good and extortionately expensive consultant will tell you, I responded with two simple words: 'it depends'.

A word of advice

'It depends' — always remember these words when someone is trying to test or force you into a statement of position.

I am a firm believer that every situation has unique characteristics that can vary greatly. My wife says that I sit on the fence at times, and maybe she's right. Although I can be extremely opinionated, I do believe that it's naive to race into a hard-and-fast view of a situation without clearly understanding the key facts at hand.

Back to Peter and his interview question. Following my masterful opening gambit, I proceeded to ramble badly and continued with something like this: 'Well, it depends on what country, time and specific situation you're in. The English probably rate logic first, with law and relationships on an equal footing. In countries like Italy and France relationships probably trump all. Old Eastern Bloc regions are generally dictated by law, and maybe North America is starting to follow that direction as well'. I almost bore myself when I think back to my long-winded response.

As you have possibly gathered, Peter had likely seen this a hundred times before. The young 'try-hard' executive trying to sound clever and totally missing the point. Regardless of anything I was going to come out with, Peter wasn't asking a question; he was doing what good leaders and great mentors do. He was making a point.

In essence, his point (which I only realised years later) was this: 'it doesn't matter where you have come from, what you have heard or even experienced. In business, relationships matter more than anything else. Regardless of changes in law and logic, relationships will always be the most important asset'.

Maybe you could argue this point with me.

You could present historical charts linked to specific changes in legislation and correlate them against actual performance — you could show systematic changes in decision making that avoid the pitfalls of human bias, error or emotion. In fact, if you were being particularly cutting, you could rebut with those two magic words, 'it depends'.

Either way, my response would be the same as Peter's that day: I would listen, smile politely and nod with understanding. I would also look forward to seeing you in a couple of years when experience had changed your view.

The reason I tell this story is that, from my perspective, this concept remains unequivocally true. Despite living in a world of hard scientific data, exploding levels of AI and machine learning, and ever increasing red tape and regulation, the importance of relationships still remains paramount.

Without respectful connections between relevant parties, sustained mutual success will always be an impossibility. We see daily evidence of this. Transformational strategies fall short of their vision and innovative solutions fail at execution — they come up short not because they lack logic or legality. They fail because of low levels of trust, understanding and genuine care among disparate groups of individuals. They fail because of failed relationships.

The big question: if relationships are so critical for success, why are we so far from mastering them? I have three theories.

The first is that it's easier to focus on law and logic than on relationships. Law and logic are both known; they are black and white, and have set rules, defined end points and encompass degrees of certainty. Relationships are anything but.

Secondly, many people feel that their work and results alone will do the talking and believe their success can be achieved in isolation. This way of thinking is flawed and limits potential.

Finally, there is an absence of effective models on how to become a relationship builder. The adjective 'effective' is key to this point: if there were effective models in existence, they would already be followed and I would not be writing this chapter.

Law, logic, relationships. Thank you, Peter: exceptional coaching.

THE PRACTICAL PART

Some steps to mastering relationships

Although they are never easy to achieve, relationship skills are a necessity for corporate success. I use the following framework (see figure 1.1) to build interpersonal skills. The drivers are self-evident, yet the specific behaviours are what bring it alive. As with all competencies, they require dedicated focus and should remain constant 'to work on' items. Good luck.

Drivers	Behaviours
Believe	Personal first
	Early vulnerability
Focus	Day one trust
	Uncomfortable comfort
Deliver	Recognise and reward
	Time and space
Repeat	Acknowledge

Figure 1.1: mastering relationships — a framework of simplicity

Drivers

- **Believe.** Value relationships ahead of both law and logic. If you already believe, move to the next steps. If you do not, do me a favour. Revisit this chapter after closely observing what constitutes the success of outstanding people, initiatives and businesses. Dig deep and seek out the exceptional.

- **Focus.** I regularly tell our middle child, Oscar, that 'you can do anything in this world, but you can't do everything'. Focus is a choice that you can only make with real commitment. Dedicate at least 50 per cent of personal development to mastering relationship skills. It may feel self-indulgent; it is not. Don't stop doing the functional stuff, but relationship-building must come first.

For existing leaders, ensure you act with immediacy on those who demonstrate poor relationship behaviours. Never tolerate them and never tolerate repeated negative behaviours. It will signal low importance for interconnectivity across your organisation, a very dangerous message to send.

- **Deliver.** Do it authentically or don't do it at all. Never achieve through manipulation or enter a relationship for individual gain. I am ashamed to say I have done this in the past. Unless you build on enduring trust and respect, you will fail. In chapter 6, I talk about how you can develop your own leadership style and your own leadership brand. This is critical.

- **Repeat.** Do not become complacent with relationships. As with personal connections, they need constant attention. Once you have a model that works for you, try to move from success to mastery. Success means one-off wins, while mastery means continual fulfilment, time and time again.

Behaviours

- **Personal first.** I start my interactions on a personal basis and then move on to business. It does not work with everyone and often I will have limited time to make this a reality. Being genuinely inquisitive about others' backgrounds, interests and passions goes a long way to establishing trust. Personally, I always feel appreciated and valued when others take the time to do it with me.

- **Early vulnerability.** In every relationship, I will attempt to be transparent, honest, and, where appropriate, vulnerable. To me, this is the hallmark of enduring partnerships.

- **Day one position of trust.** Most people have one of two trust models. I give complete trust from day one and it only disappears if that trust is broken. I do this for the quickest path to breakthrough transformation. This may be perceived as naive, and at times I will be let down by others. It is a sacrifice I have accepted and intuition through experience serves me well. The alternate model is having to earn trust before it is given. Neither model is correct, just different.

- **Comfortable with the uncomfortable.** This is a massive skill if mastered early. I have always raised my hand for leadership roles, assignments and projects that test my relationship skills. Especially the challenging ones.

- **Recognise and reward.** Start recognising and rewarding those who are strong relationship builders. Place people who are connectors and integrators as leads on cross-functional assignments — even if they know little about the subject matter. Above all, talk loudly to others about the value they bring to the organisation. It is not easy to be or develop into a great relationship builder, so support them fully.

- **Time and space.** Allow your teams the opportunity to create and build harmony among themselves. Some people conduct team-building exercises. Personally, they drive me nuts. My preference is for agendas that create heaps of space for personal interaction, the majority being away from a business setting and, preferably, over a drink or two. I used to underestimate the value of this, as I could not see an immediate and definable return. I now realise I was very naive to think like this.

- **Acknowledge.** I have quickly realised that not everyone is a great integrator of others. If you derive energy from being an individual contributor, who am I to say otherwise? If this is you at your best, then I should not change you. I just need to ensure that you have the right role and the right fit for the organisation. We all have different skill sets, and each has value.

MODELS FOR THE WHITEBOARD

Trust Preference model

I like the simplicity of this model (see figure 1.2).

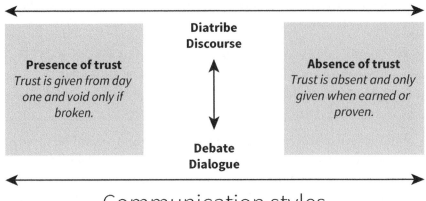

Figure 1.2: trust preferences — a personal choice

It sums up the preferences of trust that most of us have — you either give it immediately or wait until it is earned. At times we may vacillate between the two, but, generally, most of us will have a clear predisposition. Once trust levels are established, then the magic of partnership begins. Conversations will move from a one-way flow of information, *diatribe* and *discourse*, to a two-way flow — *debate* and *dialogue*. Importantly, they also move from positions of conflict to positions of cooperation. If you are interested in further reading, there is a quirky cat named David W. Angel who shares some very cool models on this alongside general conflict resolution, 'the four stages of conversation' in particular (www.davidwangel.com).

External Connections model

Remember the big debate of vertical versus horizontal integration? Ownership and control versus specialisation by others? There was never a clear winner. What is obvious today is the necessity for external partnership and connectivity. The modern corporate world demands connectivity, and, in its absence, it is almost impossible to achieve true breakthrough. Particularly if you want to do so with real pace and efficiency. This framework (see figure 1.3) is a good reminder of why external connectivity is so important, alongside simple reminders of how to achieve it. I have provided specific details on my website, www.hamishrthomson.com. Definitely refer to it when conducting stretch assignments outside your organisation's core competency sets.

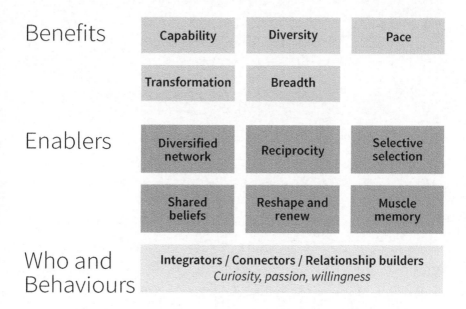

Figure 1.3: External Connections model for breadth and breakthrough in partnerships

THE CRITIQUE

A brief review from one of Australasia's pre-eminent lawyers and cultural experts, Joydeep Hor, Founder and Managing Principal, People + Culture Strategies, Sydney, Australia.

It would be heretical to most lawyers to have one of their own extol the virtue and importance of relationships over logic, and certainly over law! However, I had to smile when I read this chapter because it paraphrases a model that I have used for all of my professional work since I started my career 23 years ago.

One of the catalysts for setting up my own firm was that the clients I served were dealing with their people problems through a very specific lens. For most organisations, their focus was on 'commerce' (business effectiveness) and 'law' (legal compliance). Essentially, 'How can we get rid of this person from our organisation whom we consider to be counter-cultural or not adding value, but do it in a manner that doesn't get us into legal hot water?'

I soon realised that for most organisations this mindset was not only a short-term, firefighting approach to people management, but one that was actually working against them in terms of being even remotely strategic or being an 'engaging' employer. Often the consequences for the organisations embracing this mindset were

- considerable adverse publicity

- high turnover

- a range of other undesirables.

They may well be achieving a 'solution' to what they thought their problem was, but it was only giving rise to other problems elsewhere or not addressing the core underlying issue.

The model I developed follows a quadrant methodology. It suggests that in addition to 'commerce and law', organisations need to explicitly consider the areas of 'psychology' and 'sociology'. In other words, for them to be better at people management, they need to reflect genuinely on the question of what their people are thinking and feeling and how their organisation's decision might look as a result.

Relationships as a part of organisational and people effectiveness underpins this entire philosophy. Every aspect of our firm's advice and guidance follows this belief. This may range from how to handle a bullying complaint or how to deal with an underperforming employee to how to introduce major change in organisations. It has universal relevance.

In closing, I should also say that as a professional services provider, the importance of relationships (business and personal) with our clients is overarching. A transactional approach to service provision may see short-term gains, but is a guaranteed recipe for longer term unsustainability. Merely being a good lawyer or adviser is the price of entry: clients have too much at stake to be satisfied with that alone. They need people in their extended team to have a deep understanding of who they are and what they value, and then advise and guide them with a single-minded focus on making them better at those things.

Chapter 2
Drains and Radiators

Life is too short to be surrounded by negative people. In fact, life is too short to not be surrounded by positive people. When we are surrounded by positivity, exceptional things happen. When we are surrounded by negativity, average things happen.

American essayist Ralph Waldo Emerson wrote, 'People do not seem to realise that their opinion of the world is also a confession of their character'. I couldn't agree more.

Unacceptably, but invariably, we seem to allow negative people to populate our world. We do it all the time, and I just don't get it.

Transcendentalists, of which Emerson was one, believe that one should rely upon intuition rather than reason or logic; that spontaneous feelings are superior to deliberate intellectualism. Transcendentalism also greatly values optimism.

I think I would have liked Emerson.

He was a true radiator in every sense.

THE MESSAGE ························

Here is an age-old question for you: does happiness lead to success or does success lead to happiness?

There is a multibillion-dollar industry that now exists to answer that question. It's science, psychology and academia rolled into one, art, self-discovery and spirituality united. Pursuit of happiness (encompassing life coaching and self-help, among others) is big business, and a noble one at that.

You are likely familiar with the concept of employee engagement. If it's not termed 'engagement', then odds on it will be called 'satisfaction', 'culture', or even just a plain old 'pulse' survey. Regardless, most organisations subscribe to one of these concepts at one stage or another. Big money is spent and considerable hours are devoted, all in the name of making us infinitely happier.

I'm not going to bad-mouth these programs or surveys. I've taken part in them throughout my entire career. Most times I've enjoyed them, and many times I have benefited from them.

But if I was pushed into a corner and asked what I would do if left to my own devices, well, I wouldn't choose a survey. I wouldn't spend countless hours on analysis, discovery sessions or 'feeling' forums. I wouldn't create team action plans or even dot colourful motivational posters throughout the office. No, it would be a lot simpler than that.

I would choose to surround myself with radiators and avoid drains like the plague. That's what I would do.

···

There is much debate on the origins of the drains and radiators concept. Various people, companies and indeed countries have claimed to be the originators of the drains and radiators story. What I do know for certain is it did not come from me.

However, I unashamedly refer to this concept on a regular basis. It perfectly resonates with me and has made a big difference to my success and happiness over the years.

So, what is it all about?

Essentially, there are two types of people in the world: drains and radiators. We are surrounded by them. Friends, family, colleagues, neighbours, high achievers, down-and-outers and just about anyone else we can think of.

Drains do exactly what they say. They drain. They drain the energy out of things. They suck out the lifeblood of possibility, they restrict opportunity, they halt progress and they inevitably snatch defeat from the jaws of victory. They are individuals who see life through a 'glass half empty' lens. They are people who inflict negativity on not only themselves but everyone around them.

Don't get me wrong, we all have occasional drain moments, and I'm no exception. But we're not talking about infrequent lapses. We're talking about the people who drain you of energy, day in and day out. Maybe you're even one of them yourself.

Radiators, on the other hand, do exactly what they say they do. They radiate. They are a spark of energy and a source of positivity. We feel warm around radiators. They are shining lights of inspiration. They exude possibility and have a can-do attitude that is infectious. Above all else, when they are next to you, you stand that much taller.

If you're a clever cookie who refutes this concept, let me get in early. Four things:

1. I'm not talking of a 'Pollyanna', one of those blind optimists who find the good in everything while basing that opinion on nothing.

2. I'm not saying that a challenger, provocateur or stereotypical 'hard-arse' chief financial officer should be labelled a drain. Far from it. Diversity of thought is invaluable, as is rigorous debate to test and challenge our convictions. No, I will never underplay the importance of a provocateur, as they are always necessary to keep us on our toes.

3. There will always be drains who are wealthy and successful. It is a numbers game and there are many examples to prove it. Sometimes, the very negative nature of someone's personality will

lead them to riches. Good for them, and if it works, go forth. For me, though, buggered if I ever want to be one and I definitely do not want to hang out with them. Life has more than enough hassles as it is.

4. There are probably lots of neutral people out there, but 'neutral' and 'average' do not make a good concept in the world of marketing or advertising. This concept is pretty much legendary within all ad agencies and when you explain it to anyone, they can relate even though they of course know that it can't be that black and white. It's like saying, in terms of US politics, that you are either a Republican or a Democrat — yet we know there are so many variations in between.

Aside

There are many companies that employ a standardised process to ensure that challenge and rigorous debate takes place on all major decisions. I talk in chapter 8, Bad bosses are great bosses, about a former boss who used to play the devil's advocate on every single subject raised. It was relentless. Regardless of the position you put across, even if he agreed with it, he would argue the alternate black and blue.

About two years after he had retired from the business he casually mentioned his approach to me. The bit that I had not realised — and I was not alone on this — was that this behaviour was 100 per cent intentional. Even if he 'fully agreed' with your hypothesis, he would challenge you.

I still don't know if I agree with this approach. I certainly did not support the manner in which he challenged people, however my conviction on my stances was never stronger than it was under his leadership. My preparation was more comprehensive and, as a result, I was infinitely better prepared for eventual execution. Another example of an invaluable lesson that I did not appreciate at the time. (Maybe it was just me who needed to grow up a bit?)

I also had a colleague who worked with former mining company Xstrata (now part of Glencore PLC). For every major decision that was to be made by senior management, they demanded that they see fully fledged alternates. The interesting part was that these alternates had to be extremities placed at the very edges of a 'four-quadrant' option model. Only provocative and challenging extremities were accepted, and, unless they were given true thought leadership and diligence (i.e., were not just treated as a tick-box exercise), they would be sent back for repeated investigation. I like this approach. It makes the standard format of appointing someone to play the 'bad cop' on your leadership team look a little undercooked at best.

Yes, we will always need challengers of substance.

Back to drains and radiators. The original story I have been told goes as follows.

The CEO of an advertising agency — which I will not name, but think large, major and global — called his entire team together for one extraordinary meeting. He stood alone at the top of the stairs with all his creative disciples below. With clarity and eloquence he proceeded to explain what was meant by both a drain and a radiator. Fairly standard descriptions and definitions. Prior to concluding, as all good leaders do, he made a call to action:

'I only want radiators in this agency. If you are a radiator, you will go far. Very far. If you happen to be a drain, however, well it's pretty simple. You can fuck off and you can fuck off now.'

He smiled, walked off and went back to his office. Nothing more was said.

Who knows if it went down like that? Nonetheless, since hearing the story, I have communicated the drains and radiators concept to every team I have had the privilege to lead. Sometimes using the same colourful language, but hopefully always with a slightly more inspiring tone!

NEGATIVITY HURTS

The radiator versus drain analogy relates as much to personal life as it does to business. At times, I don't mind having a drain around me. Every now and then it makes me feel good to hear someone else have a moan, gripe or bitch at the injustices of life. It's almost therapy, in some ways, to think that I'm not alone in having such negative thoughts.

That said, for me, I only want to indulge such negativity on an occasional basis. On a personal front, I think most of us are pretty selective when it comes to the type of people we surround ourselves with when outside of work. Time for social interaction is always limited so when we do get the chance to kick back, the last thing we want is for others around us to be negative. Sometimes, drains cannot be avoided, yet the older I get, I am certainly doing my best to ensure we have more radiators surrounding the Thomson clan.

In a work environment I can think of nothing worse than having drains around me. In fact, there is worse: having drains around the rest of my team. To have negative people sucking the energy out of you and others is just toxic. Some of my most frustrating meetings have pertained to future vision and strategic planning sessions. When they go well, they are some of the most inspirational and motivational days you will have within your career. I love them. At times though, they can be uncommonly depressing, filled with:

- individuals with pre-determined 'limiting' beliefs

- people with 'impossible to forget' or 'never can be changed' historical experiences

- creators of inadvertent roadblocks at every turn

- those with inadequate thirst for curiosity and perspective

- the occasional team member who just thinks it's a waste of time to think 'possibility'.

I have little time for these behaviours, and, when they manifest within a team environment, they spread like wildfire.

Like most, when I look back at my career to date, I wish I had moved faster in removing drains from my places of work. Right now, I can think of three specific senior leaders that I encountered, humoured and even supported for way too many years. They were undeniably drains. In each instance, I had the opportunity to do something about it and, regretfully, I didn't act with pace. I should have removed them quickly and shielded my teams and the business from their pessimism. Each of them was functionally strong, yet it was inexcusable that I let that cloud my judgement. With those individuals I did move on quickly, not once have I had a regret — and, speaking to many of them over the years, I've found it was the right call for them and the business. For the organisations and team cultures that I wanted to create, their outlook wasn't the right fit.

Conversely, there is a great line that I was exposed to recently: 'I have never fired someone for having too much passion.' Wise words.

A word of advice

There are numerous scientific studies showing the health and psychological benefits of positivity. Positive thinking has been correlated with improved immunity, reduced levels of stress, anxiety and negative, intrusive thoughts, coupled with general happiness and a reduction in unhealthy behaviours. When a radiator next asks me for a pay rise, maybe I should remember the above!

LEADERSHIP ENERGY

A few years back I attended a CEO industry forum with James Allen (co-author of *The Founder's Mentality*) from Bain & Company consulting. He talked at length about the number one asset that he believes a CEO can possess. In his mind, it was 'energy.'

The energy of a great leader can radiate throughout an organisation and set the foundation for true cultural change. I often remind myself of this. Despite being conscious of getting the right people on and off the bus, I need to start with myself. If I am not setting a tone of opportunity and possibility, or bringing maximum energy every day into the office, then I am not doing my position justice. For every leader, this can be demanding. My most recent boss never appeared to have an off day. She was always on top of her game and, despite difficult challenges, she never dropped her intensity or energy levels. I am in awe of this. (I outline tactical approaches for energy management in chapter 11, Get a life. They are instrumental lessons.)

THE PRACTICAL PART

This is slightly different from the other chapters.

This framework will not inform you 'how' to become a radiator; rather, it will assist in identifying them and how to flush out the drains.

The 30 per cent rule

Radiators love this concept; drains fear it. The 30 per cent rule is to facilitate needed behavioural change. In this framework, stretch targets are set to such a level that individuals and teams have no chance of achieving them unless they do things differently. Depending on micro and macro factors, this stretch target could be 10, 30 or even 70 per cent above current levels.

I use this rule regularly within both mid- and long-term strategic planning to dictate necessary change. (It should not be used for those areas of the business that require continuous improvement. 'Sweating the assets' and optimising efficiency and operations will always be key, but that is a different target-setting exercise.)

This framework (see figure 2.1) is largely self-explanatory.

When followed, radiators will usually rise to the top and, fortunately, drains will flush away.

Harsh, but true.

The 30 per cent rule

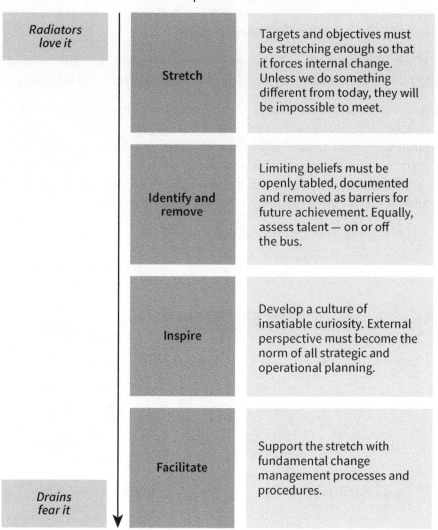

Radiators love it	**Stretch**	Targets and objectives must be stretching enough so that it forces internal change. Unless we do something different from today, they will be impossible to meet.
	Identify and remove	Limiting beliefs must be openly tabled, documented and removed as barriers for future achievement. Equally, assess talent — on or off the bus.
	Inspire	Develop a culture of insatiable curiosity. External perspective must become the norm of all strategic and operational planning.
Drains fear it	**Facilitate**	Support the stretch with fundamental change management processes and procedures.

Figure 2.1: the 30 per cent rule — dictating behavioural change

MODELS FOR THE WHITEBOARD

Igniting Change Management

When undertaking significant change programs within your organisation, it is essential you enlist the support of influential radiators.

As I'm sure you're aware, there are multiple change management models in existence. This one is via US-based strategic consultants Triangle Strategy Group. It has helped me to overcome limiting beliefs and perceived barriers to transformational agendas. The three specific areas detailed here garner my attention: two require the brilliance of radiators and the last requires a pragmatic realist. I like this balance.

Figure 2.2 is an abridged version of the model.

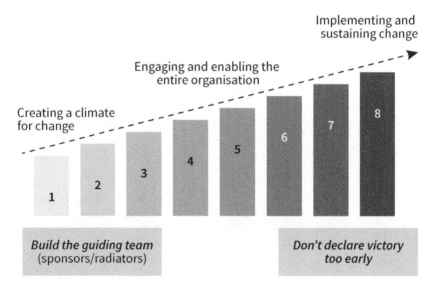

Figure 2.2: change management — a radiator's playground

- **Create a climate or catalyst for change.** The best way to do this is to light a fire. Usually a large one. It has to have impact and it should be done early, before your team is being forced into change. Do this by using the clarity of numbers and facts. As an example, calling out a clearly unacceptable annual profit position and its likely impact on business stability (i.e., our jobs) will usually get immediate attention. This is not a threat position, it's simply reality. When co-delivered by well-respected and well-liked radiators, even tough communications can result in positive outcomes.

  Do not go in soft when communicating a burning platform.

- **Get the right sponsors on board. (Radiators, of course.)** I have learned the hard way on this topic. What seems obvious to you is never as clear-cut to others. The well-versed proverb says it best: 'If you want to go fast, go alone. If you want to go far, go together'.

  Before you even contemplate communicating your change agenda, get the right sponsors on board and make sure they are radiators. This may sound political, and maybe it is. But it works.

- **Don't declare victory too early.** This is where the pragmatic realist comes in. As soon as victory is declared, tension valves are reduced across an organisation. Complacency can set in, which often results in a downward spiral of performance.

  Be aware, this is not just the mistake of rookie managers. Leaders of all levels declare victory way too early. I have definitely been guilty of this, but fortunately my constant state of dissatisfaction keeps me grounded on this one.

Talent Identification

For an alternate lens to recruit and attract radiators, let me share with you a formula (shown in figure 2.3) that the head of one of Australasia's largest communications agencies shared with me. It goes like this:

Curiosity + willingness > experience

It remains one of my few useful algebra equations.

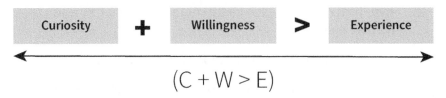

Figure 2.3: talent identification — an alternate lens

Although I am not completely aligned to the theory — after all, I have devoted an entire chapter to how undervalued experience actually is (chapter 7, Ever heard of Harry Redknapp?) — I cannot help but resonate with its sentiments.

Even without subject matter experience, outstanding integrators, connectors and radiators can be 'game changers' to an organisation. Providing they have insatiable curiosity, passion and a willingness to learn, they can be amazing conductors of energy and respective productivity.

Although there will always be some operational roles where experience will be mandatory (never compromise on these), if new models like this one bring more radiators into my teams, then I will always be a supporter.

Thank you, Nick — a great alternate lens to consider.

THE CRITIQUE

A brief review from global advertising executive Leif Stromnes, Managing Director, Strategy and Innovation, DDB Australia.

....

When you work in advertising for 30 years, and survive, and maybe even thrive, you have to have thick skin, and maybe be a bit delusional, even Pollyanna-ish sometimes.

Our business is one that doesn't really make sense. It can't, because it's entirely emotional. In fact, the best advertising doesn't make sense — until it does.

While our clients are taught to manage risk, we're in the business of encouraging them to risk everything for the sake of fame and being noticed. Because that's how advertising works. If you don't get noticed, everything else is academic.

Ours is a business of planned chaos, of accidental collisions among people with deep and wide mental pantries. And, if we're lucky, good ideas emerge. I have never seen a linear 'route one' path to good advertising. The process to getting to a thing called an idea is ambiguous, stop-start, confrontational and downright terrifying at times.

So how do we make it work? By surrounding ourselves with creative and clever people who radiate good energy and radical positivity. People who make stuff happen, and who won't easily take no for an answer. They can be prickly bastards at times, but they are doing what it takes to create great work.

And it begins at the top. Every industry and business has a rainmaker, a pivotal person who makes the place what it is. In advertising, it's the executive creative director. There's a reason they are paid more than the CEO: they *are* the business. They are the keepers of the secret sauce, the mythical dark art. And they make miracles happen on a daily basis.

I was schooled on this when I had just started out in advertising and was working for a multinational agency. Our global head of creativity was on a world tour and we were instructed to assemble in the boardroom for his presentation.

He was fantastic! Funny, rude, obnoxious and audacious. He walked in and you could just feel the creativity.

He told the most brilliant story. He said to succeed in advertising you had to tell everyone about your dreams and hopes. Because advertising was full of dreamers, people who were risking everything to do something worthwhile. It was 1995, and *Toy Story* was a global hit for Pixar. He played a video that I will never forget. In the video he is standing in a g-force suit in what looked like snowy Russia. He climbs into a MiG fighter jet and gives an ironic thumbs up before his contorted face is thumped back into his seat with the forward thrust of the jets. You could hear a pin drop as this silent video played out. In the video you see him struggling to undo his suit and then he takes something out. It's the unmistakeable figurine of Buzz Lightyear. Struggling against the extreme g-forces, he lets Buzz go. And the most incredible thing happens. In zero gravity, with mach 4 thrust, Buzz Lightyear flies perfectly across the cockpit with that silly grin on his face.

'The moral of the story?' he told the stunned audience. 'Buzz Lightyear believed he could fly, and he flew.'

I fell in love with the business at that moment. And I realised what it would take to succeed.

Chapter 3

The Man Who Used to Smile

I find this image fascinating.

It is not about the former president. At best, he is a mere distraction. It's about his partner, former first lady Michelle Obama.

On so many occasions, our partners or friends are the driving force behind our success and, importantly, our own self-awareness. Those who know us tend to notice our behavioural changes way before we do.

After every leadership summit, every coaching, mentoring or self-discovery retreat that I've been on (and in a large corporate, you get sent on a lot), I'll share some new insight I've learned with my wife, and she'll say the following: 'How many times have I told you that?'

It is a thankless task, being a partner. If only we listened to them more.

Bear with me, Maddie, I will get better.

THE MESSAGE ··························

Exceptional coaches cut through.

There's no mucking around; they say it as it is. My business coach of choice is a chap called Jack Jefferies. Jack is a Colorado-based former US national skydiving team member, and he has a split personality that just seems to work: a true adventure junkie who is up for anything coupled with being one of the most professional and intellectual cookies I have ever encountered. Jack once talked to me about attitudes. He said that 'an attitude can be changed in a nanosecond. If you don't like what you're doing, you have two choices: you either change what you do, or you change your attitude. If you choose the latter, do it now.'

I have needed to change my attitude a few times over the years.

Each time, it related to needing to 'chill the fuck out'. I had stopped being the authentic me and had started taking life — well, work — way too seriously. The stress pill had been swallowed and I didn't like it.

Many of us fall into this trap. While going above and beyond is honourable — and will always be needed and valued throughout your career — the day we lose our joie de vivre is the day we need an intervention, and a quick one at that.

If you are a hard-nosed, no-nonsense, driven person, do not think this doesn't apply to you. As a leader or future leader of others, you need to ensure that your people are at their best every single day. Unless they are, you will never get the most from them. Ensuring that they get an optimal balance of what I term the 'chill zone' will enable this. This zone can never be achieved in isolation — it is equally what works for an individual and what is needed by the organisation. A difficult yet necessary balance.

And if you're a grumpy bugger who used to smile, well, we need to change. Life is way too short to be miserable. Just ask your partner.

···

This topic hurts. It disappoints (and in some ways annoys me) that I have fallen into this trap on multiple occasions. Three, in fact. Each time, I've needed to take a chill pill. That's what pains me the most: once is okay, maybe twice is acceptable — but three times having this issue? Well, it just sucks. Let me tell you about the one that made me wake up.

REALITY BITES

When I was 27, I was based in the Netherlands and had been given a significant gig looking after European marketing and communications for Reebok Europe. In many ways it was my dream job. Heaps of freedom and responsibility, energetic teams and passionate people around me, large budgets to work with, all located in one of the coolest places that a young bloke could be based. Particularly for a chap who had given it a rather 'large nudge' throughout his last dozen or so party years.

One day I was in my favourite part of Amsterdam, the central and trendy district of Jordaan, with a group of friends. I love this place: it's got a really cool vibe, with narrow canals and streets flanked by indie boutique stores, groovy little pubs and hip eateries. We used to venture there a lot — to this day it remains our port of call whenever we return to the Netherlands.

Memory tells me we were in a bar, but the Dutch have a lot of 'coffee shops', so best if we just move on. A good Scottish mate of mine, Colin, walked over with his new girlfriend and soon-to-be wife. He leaned in and said to her, 'I would like to introduce you to Hamish. The man who used to smile.'

Wow. I was not expecting that. I had always prided myself on being a reasonably chilled-out type of cat. Despite being driven and competitive, I am firmly at my best when I am relaxed. I am a massive perceiver who loves flexibility and spontaneity and the thought of not being a 'smiler' did not sit well with me.

After a bit of small talk, chatting about how wonderful Colin was and his exemplary behaviour with previous girlfriends, I pulled him aside and calmly asked the question that you can always ask a mate: 'What the hell do you mean?!'

His message was clear. 'You've been in this new gig for six months now. You've lost that old Hamish spark and take things way too seriously. You're all work and results, politically correct and definitely not the man you used to be. You don't even smile much, anymore.'

As detailed in chapter 13, Bring on the grilling, I have had some tough feedback and serves over the years. Each have hurt in their own right, yet few come close to the six words Colin had said that night: 'The man who used to smile.'

Bugger.

This wasn't me. This wasn't what had got me where I was, and this was definitely not the person I wanted to be. Since that experience (and the ones that have followed), I am firm in my conviction that I never want to be known as Hamish Thomson, that corporate bloke.

Work is one part of me. It's an important part, but not the main part. Being labelled a 'serious, uptight, intense chap' was painful. I make out that I don't care what others think of me and that it's only what I think of myself that matters. That's what self-assured people do, right?

Well, deep down, I think I'm like most people. Perceptions do matter, and, when they come from people you trust and value, they have impact. I am yet to meet anyone (apart from maybe a 'sociopath called Rod' from university — which is another book entirely) who didn't feel something similar.

What made the situation even worse was the context I was in.

I was a young guy living in Amsterdam, recently married to someone way out of my league. Pulling in some good cash, with a flash company car and all the perks of an expat assignment. Dream job with access to sporting events around the world. Great work mates and a constant influx of family and dodgy school friends visiting monthly from New Zealand. *The man who used to smile*. What the heck was I thinking?

WHERE I WENT WRONG

Before talking about what changed, I want to tell you why I got into this position in the first place. It's a common story.

The perceived importance of my new job went to my head. Nothing more, nothing less. I altered my persona pretty much the day that I started the new gig — correction, the very day that I was told I had the job.

It was a substantial promotion. My responsibilities were broader and more encompassing. Some people who had been my peers would now be my subordinates. I was going to be exposed to and working with a whole new set of people, starting fresh with limited relationships and little knowledge of my previous accomplishments.

Additionally, I changed because I assumed that was how people acted and behaved in more senior positions. Maybe this was the 'imitation factor' that I mention in chapter 8. Or, more likely, I just got my assumption horribly wrong.

As a result, I took it all too seriously. I doubled down on my hours; my fitness took a hammering; my mates took a back seat. My social life suffered and, unacceptably, my wife was very much alone, driving in the front seat.

A word of advice

While there are many great tips for commencing a new job, I have three in particular that are relevant here.

1. Never get into 'prove mode'

You have already been appointed into the role and you have nothing to prove. The hard work has been done and you should be starting from a position of total trust and credibility. If anything, others should be proving to *you* that you've joined the right company and the right team. If you do get into prove mode, you will:

- place undue pressure on yourself

- be more prone to providing 'yes' answers rather than offering challenge and perspective

- become distracted during some of the best learning periods of your career (this is the worst of all).

Please do not forget this.

2. Do not wait for answers from above

It's a natural tendency to believe that our boss, or those above them, have all the answers. That all correct decisions will be forthcoming from the wise heads of the powers that be.

They do not. Do not wait for direction, do not be shy on coming forward with views and observations, and under no circumstances should you avoid action through inertia. Leaders at all levels need fresh eyes, fresh perspective and fresh challenge. New starters provide this opportunity.

A case in point: whenever I have started a new position — regardless of whether I'm with the same organisation or a completely new one — I have always written down my initial hypotheses on the likely challenges at hand. Rightly or wrongly, I do this prior to starting the role. They are my uneducated, untainted and unbiased assumptions of the opportunities and challenges that I feel are relevant to the business and what I think is needed to address them.

I do appreciate that this sounds dangerous and potentially a little naive or arrogant. Rest assured, I do not act upon my ideas with reckless abandon, but I do use them as a starting base for further exploration and education. I mention this because, over time, I have found that the overwhelming majority of these initial assumptions have turned out to be correct.

A totally new perspective is invaluable to an organisation, and one's initial intuition should never be undervalued or underplayed. Equally, where my hypotheses have proven to be correct, they have allowed an accelerated path of execution. This alone has been of massive benefit.

I have also got into the habit of looking back at my initial list whenever I leave a position. I get a sense of validation and confidence that fuels me for the next challenge. As could be expected, there have been times when I look back and see my observations were just plain wrong. This is totally okay. I find it more frustrating when I look at original hypotheses that are still relevant and realise that I have done nothing about them. These hurt.

In the majority of cases, the reason for inaction is simply that I became immersed and indoctrinated within existing ways of working. Effectively, I became brainwashed with limiting beliefs around what is and what is not possible. The longer you're within a role or a company, the greater is the danger of this happening. It's only natural, but definitely something to watch out for and a reminder to surround ourselves with 'outside in' perspective.

3. Go at your own pace

In essence, this means you decide if you want to go in hard and fast and drive for results from day one. Or, you might decide to take more of a back seat over your first three months, observe, reflect and learn. There is no right or wrong and you will more than likely get a firm steer from your manager. But it's important to go with the approach that gives you the energy and motivation that you need within a new gig. This is an important one to get right from day one, so I advise you to take it seriously.

The other thing I remember doing while in this serious mode was 'not celebrating'. Up until that point, whenever I had been fortunate enough to secure a new job, promotion or assignment, I would celebrate! I would never big-note it around others, but I would allow myself that sense of personal satisfaction and a beer or 12.

Jack Welch, legendary former CEO of GE, talked about the importance of celebration, of enjoying the moment of satisfaction that comes with a promotion. Yet despite me coaching and mentoring so many others on this very lesson, the older I have become, the less I have done it myself. I give myself a few hours of contentment and then my thoughts turn to what's ahead: the challenges, the demands, the next steps. 'Can I do this, will I make a difference, is it possible to be as good as the person before me?' Yep, classic imposter syndrome.

What's really interesting, though, is that with every increased role or assignment I've been given, I realise after just a few short months that it is not as daunting as I had originally feared. For sure, there are always challenges, but after a little bit of time in the saddle, so to speak, I have never questioned whether I was up to it. Not once.

THE PRACTICAL PART

This framework (see figure 3.1) has served me well.

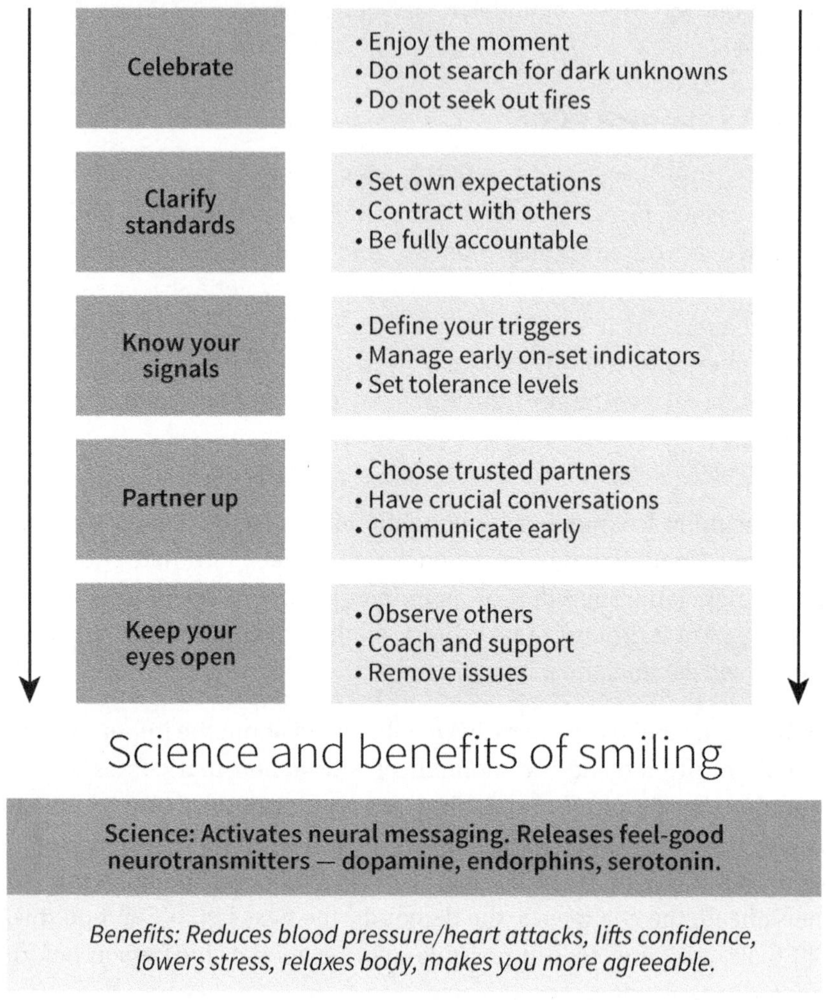

Celebrate	• Enjoy the moment • Do not search for dark unknowns • Do not seek out fires
Clarify standards	• Set own expectations • Contract with others • Be fully accountable
Know your signals	• Define your triggers • Manage early on-set indicators • Set tolerance levels
Partner up	• Choose trusted partners • Have crucial conversations • Communicate early
Keep your eyes open	• Observe others • Coach and support • Remove issues

Science and benefits of smiling

Science: Activates neural messaging. Releases feel-good neurotransmitters — dopamine, endorphins, serotonin.

Benefits: Reduces blood pressure/heart attacks, lifts confidence, lowers stress, relaxes body, makes you more agreeable.

Figure 3.1: the man who used to smile — a 5-step process

- **Celebrate** your promotions and make sure you enjoy the moment for what it is. Do not search for the dark unknowns or unseen challenges of the new role. They will come soon enough. Naturally, do advanced preparation, but do not seek out fires when you haven't lit them.

- **Clarify standards** and expectations. Your first point of clarity needs to come from you. What standards do you want to set within your current position — targets, goals and behaviours? These are the most important standards to set. You will also need to clarify those of your line manager and their expectations, however, unless you start with yourself, you will never gain full satisfaction or achievement.

Aside

Matthew Elliott, the former Panthers NRL team coach (that's Rugby League for the non-Antipodean reader), told a group of Wrigley senior executives a compelling story.

Early in the season, the Panthers found themselves in somewhat of an unusual position. They were sitting on top of the NRL ladder. They had started off the year strongly and there was a real sense of buzz and anticipation within the wider club community. Elliott was asked during a press conference if he felt any pressure from the expectations of those around him — players past and present, board members, staff and indeed the wider Panthers supporter base. His response was telling: 'Wouldn't it be a crying shame if the expectations of others were greater than my own?'

I have never forgotten this and since that day, I always define my standards and my expectations early within my tenure. Even ahead of those above me.

- **Know your signals** and early warning signs prior to the onset of 'serious' mode. What behaviours or signs do you exhibit when you start forgetting to smile?

  Probably my biggest signal is patience. Specifically, a lack of it. I have a very weak poker face in this respect.

- **Partner up** and identify 'trusted informants' who can tell it like it is. Who are those mates, colleagues or trusted family members who can give you open, direct and in-the-moment feedback? Great relationships allow crucial conversations, like the one I had with Colin, to happen.

- **Keep your eyes open** as you look for changes of behaviour in others. Not just as a leader, but as a colleague and friend. Who appears to be losing their swagger? Am I contributing to it, and what can I do to help? Early conversations with them is an outstanding start.

- **Smile.** I remember very clearly a session I had with Reckitt Benckiser when developing advertising for their Bonjela brand (at the time the UK's leading teething gel brand). They invited in one of their internal scientists who lectured us for almost two hours on the benefits of smiling.

  The science is convincing and the advantages compelling.

MODELS FOR THE WHITEBOARD

The Chill Zone

I enjoy using this model to try to get people into their ideal state of flow. It is particularly relevant when you see people on the extremities of being too serious or too relaxed and complacent. It is a ridiculously simple concept to get. I have seen versions used for both athlete training and corporate engagement. Some call it the flow zone. I term it the Chill Zone (see figure 3.2).

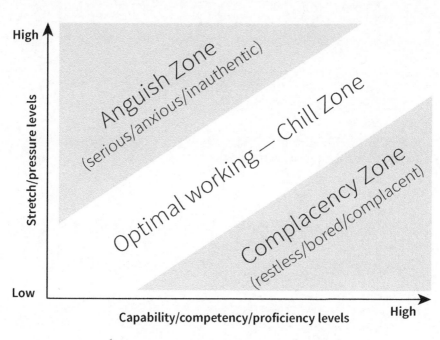

Figure 3.2: the Chill Zone — your optimal working flow

THE CRITIQUE

A brief review from Jon Burgess, international thought leader, speaker and adviser in people advocacy, connectedness and collaboration; Founder & CEO of Kwan Management Consultancy.

....

'Don't forget about the person across the table.'

I am not going to mention smiles, enjoyment or joie de vivre. Hamish's story is his own. We all have moments of significance and silence within our life and career journeys. What is defining is Hamish's friend's 'duty of care'. This is what I want to focus on — what others can do for you and what you can do for others.

When I was 15, I left Australia for England to pursue my dream of playing in the English Premier League (EPL). Naive, alone, dyslexic, with untapped ability. I ventured out with high expectations and, five years later, returned with silence. On my day, my abilities matched anyone's. My lack of confidence disallowed other days. But I do not have regrets over my experience; I have reflections.

I have built a career and a business based on connections and connectivity. Although my Harvard experience and research backs me up, I often stand alone in my conviction of their importance.

My first reflection is that I used to think that I had to be around successful people to learn, that I should seek out wisdom and experience from the very top. Yet with time I discovered that I could achieve wisdom through those who were sitting across the table from me. Every connection that fosters real trust and care provides learning; you don't need to go to the very top to get this.

My second reflection came seven years ago. It was a moment of significance. Following a lecture I had given on connectivity, a Millennial approached me and said, 'I can give you a voice when you are not there'. His offer was genuine. He liked my messaging but realised I alone could not convince the world of its importance.

Through connection, people can think of you and advocate for you when you are not there. We assess our teams and people on character and capability, not on their propensity and skills for developing and enabling connections. A miss.

My final reflection is a current one. Five-year planning cycles are a luxury. With data, digitisation and immediate shareholder return, they are now 12 months. Business appreciates the need for internal and external collaboration, and they jump straight to it, skipping the part of making connections. Of developing true reciprocity in trust, caring and curiosity that can result in break-out collaboration.

No-one survives on their own. Don't forget about the person across the table.

Chapter 4

Results Are Nice but Awards Matter

Yeah, yeah, I know. I couldn't even go a few chapters without including a photo of my All Blacks hero, Richie McCaw.

Call it a man-crush, but this guy is a legend. Humility in spades, values through the roof and a 'lead by example' work ethic that is yet to be matched. Impressive.

He, along with countless other sporting greats, have an inherent belief that the result will be the result. No point thinking too much about it, as it's how you get there that matters.

Results and awards working in perfect balance. With two consecutive Rugby World Cups and an 89 per cent All Blacks captain success ratio, there might just be something in this.

THE MESSAGE ···························

I believe there is a distinction between results and awards.

Results are numbers on a page, figures on an income statement and positions on a quantifiably measured graph. They are factually cold, hard and indisputable. As they are undeniably important, every good leader will chase them with rigour and ruthless determination.

Results create satisfaction, contentment and a sense of individual and team achievement. Like you, if you're reading this book, I value results greatly. They have driven me throughout my entire career.

Awards, on the other hand, are a level up.

Awards create a feeling of euphoria. A state of excitement and unbridled passion that radiates throughout an entire organisation. There is no better feeling than this euphoria: unified hype, buzz and energy that is palpable. Awards and recognition from others can achieve this, where results alone cannot.

Of course, results and awards are not mutually exclusive. Results will always contribute to awards. If there is no meaningful result behind an award, it will largely be viewed as worthless.

We have a problem, however.

The business world is more demanding than ever. It is a serious game with little time for sentiment. Everything is measurable and results are instantaneous. Shareholders demand consistency, repeatability and predictability, not recognition.

As a result, leaders become modest and bashful. We tend not to talk or focus on awards, as that's what other less successful companies do. Heck, as a former marketing guy, I have been guilty of this.

But just before we accept that, ask yourself one question: Do I want my organisation to experience a euphoric state of excitement that can only be achieved by recognition and award?

I do. And that is why awards matter. Way more than you think. It's time that we started taking them seriously, again.

····································

It is important that I do not get too philosophical in this chapter. Or emotional, biased or idealistic. If I am not careful, it could become an opinion piece. I will endeavour not to let this happen.

So, why should awards matter?

Firstly, science supports the benefits and importance of winning. Not just for an athlete, but for an organisation.

Cognitive neuroscientist Ian H Robertson believes that success and failure shape us more powerfully than genetics or drugs. When an individual wins a contest, there is a large release of testosterone and dopamine into their brain. Over time, these releases change brain structures and chemical makeup, making people feel smarter, better, more confident and able to take on larger challenges than ever before. The theory pertains to not only humans, but animals and fish. Robertson believes that all species have hierarchies, and that your position within that hierarchy will determine your health, mental function and mood. He coins this 'the winner effect'.

Stop and reflect on this.

If coming first actually alters brain chemistry, making people who are winners more focused, confident and assertive, what do you think happens the next time they're challenged or placed within a pressure situation? The answer is that they are more likely to succeed.

Winning is infectious. The more often you win, the more likely it is you'll win again in the future. This has been related to fields as diverse as chess, sport, business and stock trading.

There is also scientific theory that winning makes you live longer.

Nobel Prize winners outlive Nobel nominees by approximately two years. Yet both groups are unquestionably brilliant. Baseball players who make it into the Hall of Fame live longer than those mere mortals who just missed the mark. Academy Award winners live on average four years longer than their equally famous contemporary thespians.

Why else do awards matter?

AWARDS ARE TALENT MAGNETS

They attract the very best into your organisation, and, for those already there, they function as a retention strategy that is second to none. Corporate reputation and employee branding are some of the most important and growing factions within business today, yet they come with a steep price tag. The resources required to make an impact are considerable, and many of these activities, while noble, make little noticeable difference. Consider on the other hand what awards do for talent attraction and retention.

When I demand my teams recruit an unfair share of talent, there are few better levers for them to pull than showcasing awards. Exceptional people want to join exceptional businesses. They are wary of flashy and well-crafted Employee Value Propositions (EVPs) and are rightly hesitant to trust the corporate rhetoric from an HR department or charismatic CEO. What matter are the feedback and opinions of those in the know — customers, consumers, suppliers, industry and association groups and, of course, the employees themselves. (It's little wonder that global reviewer sites such as Glassdoor have risen in prominence.) And respected awards showcase exceptional organisations. Granted, there will always be some awards that are questionable, where lobbying, politics and sometimes investment levels can sway an outcome. Generally, though, these awards get found out quickly and are dismissed in the minds of most. The awards that are respected, however, make a massive difference.

A sustainability award from a national body on climate change, or a coveted Greatest Place to Work Award, or an Employee of the Year Award from your company leaders; even lesser known awards — from local community, trust barometer and entrepreneurial to functional and departmental awards — matter and are highly influential for talent and company selection. Customers, consumers, suppliers and stakeholders also look at awards through a favourable lens. Association with winning cultures is always a desirable link.

Aside

The war for talent is difficult, yet essential. In a 2016 survey of global CEOs, attracting and retaining top talent was deemed the number one issue they faced — ahead of both economic growth and competitive intensity.

It's no surprise top talent is so desirable: McKinsey have found that high performers are 400 per cent more productive than average ones. With increased role complexity, the difference can be an astounding 800 per cent.

Yet employee attraction budgets are often the first thing to go when cash is tight, so I urge you to be clever regarding talent selection. Externally recognised and valued awards are distinctive company assets. Consider them wisely.

AWARDS GIVE RISE TO BREAKTHROUGH AND TO 'SPECIAL'

You do not win awards by being average. You win awards by being distinct, compelling and ahead of the competition. You do things that others don't; most of the time you will be pushing boundaries through creativity and innovation that have not been previously explored. Awards usually reflect those who have taken risks. In my mind, calculated risk will lead to breakthrough and transformation.

AWARDS PROVIDE CLARITY OF FOCUS AND DIRECTION

By this, I am talking about placing the organisation in a mindset of servicing others. If you are chasing a customer recognition award, you focus on what matters to that customer ahead of what matters to you. When seeking recognition on sustainability, you commit to metrics that make a difference to the environment you're serving. The same applies to engagement awards, community awards, product awards and just about any award that you can think of. A service mentality is always a winning strategy.

A BOOZY LUNCH LESSON

I need to level with you. Although I said I would not succumb to opinion, I remain quite emotionally biased on this topic. From a very early stage in my career, I was exposed to and somewhat brainwashed about the importance of awards. The context: fresh-faced, naive and easily influenced, I was a 21-year-old working in the world of London advertising. I came across a senior department head who was creative, sharp-witted and extremely talented. He eventually left the agency and went client side, working with Rupert Murdoch's formerly named News International Group — now News Corp.

Over a few drinks, he talked me through a simple philosophy. It has stayed with me for life.

His message: 'Results are nice, but awards matter.' I thought it was a piss-take. Even at the age of 21, a few pints down and knowing that my marketing degree was slightly debatable versus the qualifications of my Cambridge agency colleagues, I didn't believe it. What mattered in the world was obviously tangible results. Awards were simply a nice-to-have bonus. Surely?

I will not detail the contents of the two-hour discussion that followed, but when I left that long boozy lunch, I knew only one thing: awards matter and my job was to help secure them. A lesson I haven't forgotten. (Thank you, Mr Lawlor.)

WINNING: THE DRUG OF CHOICE

There is no better feeling than winning. When I worked at Reebok, I was given a very early directive: 'If you cannot create hype internally, don't bother trying it externally'. I understood this completely.

Our tactic of choice in creating hype? Awards, and numerous ones at that.

Reebok was a leading brand in those days, a clear number one in the UK market and a challenging number two or three throughout the rest of Europe. When the team won awards — and they won a lot (advertising, product, service, customer, association and industry) — you brought the house down. Receptions had video screens and music blasting out, celebrating your win from early morning to late at night. Not at polite volumes either. It was full-on mosh-pit levels, and if you think this sounds a bit over the top, nobody ever questioned it.

When a Reebok athlete or team won a major event — from Ryan Giggs, John Daly, Shaquille O'Neal and Venus Williams to Liverpool Football Club to thousands of others — the entire office would celebrate as if it was their own sporting victory. Outdoor posters the size of a double decker bus were erected on street corners outside every office, warehouse and factory. Celebratory cards were sent to employees' homes. Offices were temporarily closed for celebrations, and not one single person would even dream of wanting to be at any other company in the world. What a buzz and what a feeling. There is a reason why many Nike associates get the swoosh tattooed on their ankles: the world of sports and fitness can be extremely compelling!

Agency days in London were exactly the same. When you won awards and new account pitches, you would celebrate like there was no tomorrow. The next morning often felt like there was no yesterday, but you get the point. And Mars and Wrigley are no different. From advertising to customer to best workplace awards, the infectious nature across an entire organisation was just so damn cool. As an employee, a manager and a leader, I was inspired. After each win I felt stronger, more confident and more determined to win again. Winning was a drug of choice and it was addictive to everyone.

RISK VS AWARDS

Knowing this, I have a question. Why have awards been pushed back so far in our agenda — sometimes off the page altogether?

Unfortunately, I think we know the reasons:

- The business world is way more serious than it has ever been, and seriousness is not necessarily a good thing for euphoria.

- The bottom line of a company appears more important than ever before.

- Everyone is accountable. Whatever gets done has accountability. If it does not, someone will be held to account.

- Everything is measurable. If it cannot be measured, it will not get done.

- If an activity fails, it is unlikely that it will be repeated, even in an amended state.

- Consistency, predictability and repeatability are mandatory.

- Risk is calculated almost to an infinite degree.

- Words like *dominant*, *destroy* and *crush* are discouraged. At times we feel almost apologetic for winning and are frowned upon if we have a mindset of refusing to lose.

Slight exaggerations, but you get the gist. As a result, awards are simply viewed as a nice-to-have, and definitely not a must-do. They gain attention every now and then but seldom feature within a leadership team's key objectives.

The interesting part, however, is that when an organisation achieves balance in chasing quantifiable results and securing recognised value-add awards, extraordinary things happen.

HOW TO WIN CANNES GLOBAL ADVERTISER OF THE YEAR

Around ten years ago, Mars Incorporated introduced a new way of working for its marketing and demand function. It was cutting edge and inspired by the work of Dr Byron Sharp and the Ehrenberg-Bass Institute in particular.

Although generally common practice today, the code questioned the validity of what people 'say they will do' versus 'what they actually do'. It also leaped headfirst into the many myths of demand, the misnomers of 'brand loyalty' and 'niche targeting' being two prime examples. If you're curious about this approach, I encourage you to start with Dr Byron Sharp's book, *How Brands Grow*. It will certainly test your initial views of marketing.

The transformation was led by the former Mars Global Chief Marketing Officer, an outstanding leader who, in my mind, led a demand revolution within the business that will be difficult for others to rival. What the new code did for results was exceptional. Frameworks, guidelines and playbooks were documented and implemented across the entire organisation, including respected and valued agency partners. The art of marketing was firmly complemented with the science of data and pragmatism. As a result, capabilities and competencies increased dramatically.

The reason I tell this story is at the time I was a regional president looking after a high-performing market. I loved this new sense of logic, efficiency and related accountability — yet I was also nervous.

Would the spark and magic of creativity and innovation be lost against a new backdrop of science and data? I liked numbers, but I equally liked magic. Many of our teams were legendary at execution; they would take direction literally, never question it, and follow guidelines with laserlike precision and execute with unrivalled brilliance. Yep, I was very nervous.

I need not have been.

At the time this revolution was going on, Bruce, the very same Global CMO, was making a direct request to every single one of his global marketing leaders and agency partners: 'I want distinctive, impactful and standout communications for our brands. Creative ideas that resonate emotionally. Yes, I will hold you to account with tangible new accountability metrics, but I expect you to deliver outstanding creative work that will deliver both'. It was one of the best combination briefs that I have seen.

Many exceptional results eventuated, but one in particular stands out. In 2012 Mars Incorporated was named Cannes Global Advertiser of the Year. An infectious euphoric buzz radiated throughout every Mars office and associate around the world — a buzz that still exists today. The power of awards. Thank you, Bruce.

THE PRACTICAL PART

No frameworks or models for this one. If you believe in this premise, you will make it work.

THE CRITIQUE

A brief review from one of Europe's leading consumer marketing experts, Matt Austin, President & GM, Hasbro Inc., Europe, Middle East & Africa.

Firstly, a confession. For most of my career I've struggled with awards. Conceptually, I can see both the internal and external value, but for me, awards have generally felt a little inauthentic. I'm very aware that this is my 'story' and I find it hard to disagree with Hamish's clear and rational argument. What could be more compelling than the collective sense of organisational euphoria that happens when your CMO arrives brandishing a Golden Lion statuette?

The inauthenticity I feel is driven by three principal factors. Firstly, awards generally come from bodies where the recipient has contributed in some way financially: an annual subscription, an entrance fee or a five-figure sum for the ceremony table. Secondly, awards are too frequently bestowed upon individuals, and often hierarchical in nature. My experience is that most great work relies on a huge amount of interdependent teamwork. Nothing kills a high-performing team culture quicker than recognising an individual as first among equals. Thirdly, as a former athlete I've always been biased towards the unambiguous cold reality of results. Win, lose or draw, the result is what it is. Myriads of individual and collective stories will sit behind the success or failure, but ultimately it's the very 'coldness' that I find comforting — in hindsight perhaps too much so.

I did say at the start that I've held this view for most of my career. Recently I've come to evolve this belief in a way that's surprised me. I moved from Mars Incorporated to lead a highly successful but much smaller confectionery business. I felt soon after arriving that the talent in the organisation was of a significantly higher calibre than should necessarily be the case given the scale of the business. My surprise was amplified when I realised that the business location was in the heartland of the UK FMCG industry. How had this organisation, with so many heavyweight players as neighbours, been able to attract and retain such an exceptionally high standard of employee? Simple. It truly was a great place to work, and they had several industry awards to prove it. As a business they embraced the award and the overall process, leveraging the employee survey to drive year on year continuous improvement. Most importantly, it felt like a great place to work. From the moment I stepped into the reception on my first day the 'smell of the place' delivered on the words of the awards brochure I had been sent during the interview process. The award felt truly authentic and all the more compelling as a result.

My leadership lesson was simple: if you're going to talk the talk, walk the walk. If your award nomination comes as a directive from above, coupled with a corporate communications playbook and appropriate social media hashtag — give it a wide birth. If the award reflects on the people who actually did the work, meets a criteria that truly mirrors your company culture, drives continuous improvement and reflects your values as a leader, embrace it, win it and celebrate the hell out of it. After all, results are important, but awards can matter too.

Chapter 5

It's Not Always Right to be Right

There are some people who like to win. Every single time.

In their minds, there is always a winner and there is always a loser. They like to control every situation and they like the power that goes with it. They need to win every single argument, discussion and debate, regardless of how big, small, important or insignificant.

As American writer and public intellectual Gore Vidal said, 'The four most beautiful words in our common language: I told you so'.

Deep down, very few of us like these people. They are annoying.

At times, I have been that person.

It does not make me proud.

THE MESSAGE ··························

I hope my tone for this chapter is slightly different from that of the others. Different because this topic is of utmost importance. It is the premise for the entire book.

It's a concept that I have struggled with on numerous occasions throughout my career. Additionally, I have witnessed many other people, at all levels, wrestle with the notion. It frustrates, confuses, annoys and distracts them. Worse still, it affects and damages relationships beyond repair, which is what concerns me.

Let me explain.

There are multiple times when you present a view or a position to another party and you get shot down for it. This hurts. It hurts even more when you genuinely believe that your position is the right one and yet, somehow, the other party still does not agree.

If the pain just stopped there, we could accept it. We feel mild frustration, yet no real damage has been done.

Unfortunately, seldom does it stop at this point. People double down and it starts to become personal. The person trying to get their position across invariably becomes more determined. They become more logical, pragmatic, factual, passionate and, eventually, more demanding and argumentative. As to the party on the receiving end, well, you know the story. They dig in their heels. They become more stubborn, more resistant, more obtuse and more closed off than before. Regardless as to what facts are being put their way, they will not budge. The longer it drags on, vacillating back and forth, with increased angst at every encounter, the greater the damage done. The relationship suffers, often irreparably.

I think most people who work in business will relate to this. If by chance you do not, it will likely have happened to you in your personal life. It's the way the human psyche works. Regardless of the evidence on the table, if someone does not like your position, has a different view or does not want to accept your stance, they will never agree with you.

There is a solution. It is not perfect. Yet it works. It involves making conscious and considered choices and involves deliberate steps. It starts with reminding yourself of the following words: 'It's not always right to be right'.

....

Paris, February 1998

I cannot be sure of the exact date, as this was a long time ago. The man who taught me this principle was Jean Jacques, Marketing Director of Reebok France. French through and through, he had stereotypical qualities that he portrayed in abundance: passion and emotion.

At the time, I was a relatively young and naive 28-year-old, trying to solve the world's problems — or at least those of Reebok Europe. We were having a senior leadership forum and I had just finished presenting to about a dozen European marketing heads. It was a proposal — something that I now call a plan — and I thought it was pretty darn good.

A word of advice

Over the past few years whenever I have pitched for additional funds, market expansion, capital funding, M&As et cetera, I purposely have not labelled them 'proposals'. I present them as 'plans'.

Language, far from being just semantics, makes a massive difference. A proposal, by definition, is exactly that: a suggestion put forward for the consideration of others. It already emphasises that the starting point for the decision-making process sits with others, not you. Conversely, a plan is much more definitive: it's a statement of firm intent. It's what we are going to do, and, regardless of who is making the end-point decision, it greatly implies that it is going ahead.

Not convinced? Consider the following examples of language when pitching for a multimillion-dollar capital investment project.

'We would like to **present a proposal** to do xyz. In order to get it up and running within three weeks we will need to allocate resources and develop capabilities. In addition, we would need to bring in a dedicated project manager to lead this for us. We need your help to make this happen.'

Versus

'We have **developed a plan** to do xyz. It will commence in three weeks' time. We have established and allocated key resources and capabilities to ensure success and have a dedicated project manager commencing on x date. We look forward to your support.'

Yes, some leaders will tell you to 'get back in your box' and await sign-off before getting ahead of yourself. A great leader, however, will love your conviction. They will immediately feel a degree of responsibility to make the decision work and will make it happen quickly. Nowadays, my teams regularly do this back to me, and it works more often than not.

My proposal was to centralise advertising creative and consolidate European media plans, essentially bringing disparate, stand-alone markets together to create economies of scale. Everyone in attendance agreed that the advertising on offer was outstanding. (If you cannot elicit emotion within sports advertising, you should not be in the game.) Additionally, with a combined regional spend, we were offering gross media efficiencies of almost 20 per cent per annum. Even for the 'not invented here' marketeers (those who are always hostile to outside ideas), this plan was nigh on impossible to resist.

Or so I thought.

I distinctly remember two comments coming from the floor. The first was from the marketing director of Ireland: 'Hamish, we are too small for you to worry about us'. A quiet put-down that only the Irish can make while still ending up being your best mate that night in the pub. (A relationship skill of which I am still envious.)

As I was contemplating my response, the Russian head jumped to his feet and called out in an almost comedic tone, 'And Hamish, we are too big for you to worry about us'. Ouch. Russia was the growth engine of Europe in those days, with daily queues of people at the doorstep of every Reebok store in the country. When they spoke, we listened.

Overall, a pretty clear message was being sent my way, if not in so many words: 'Back away, sunshine, your one-size-fits-all solution is not going to work for us. Move on — it's not happening on our watch'.

At the ensuing break, I remember being quietly perplexed as to what had gone wrong. I thought it was a pretty solid pitch. The advertising was exceptional and the efficiencies wildly compelling. Although it hadn't been tested to date, my newly formed role actually gave me the decision-making rights on this one. Call me soft, but for the benefit of long-term relationship builds, I didn't want to have to play that trump card. Not so early in my tenure, anyway.

As I was walking out for some much-needed fresh air, Jean Jacques placed a reassuring hand on my shoulder, leaned in, and looked me squarely in the eyes. I distinctly recall him having an ever-so-slight smirk on his face before saying, 'My friend, it's not always right to be right'. He turned and walked back inside, and that was it. It was one of my all-time favourite and most beneficial lessons in life.

No matter how good your proposal, plan or opportunity is — and even if you are looking to save a Frenchman a small fortune — if someone doesn't want to do it, then they just won't do it.

For a young bloke desperately wanting to make a difference, this was a very hard pill to swallow.

A word of advice

One of my earliest lessons within life came from my mother. It relates to confidence and conviction. She told me that when you have true confidence in your idea or position, you don't have to make the other person or party wrong for you to be right. Furthermore, it's important that a person can totally disagree with another's opinion without feeling that the other opinion has to be silenced. There is real power and validity in both these insights.

GETTING TO WIN–WIN

Almost a year on from this experience, I did something that was out of character for me. I took some time out to reflect.

The situation itself had worked out okay. We ended up compromising, with centralised media and advertising for MTV and Eurosport, while our three lead markets (the UK, Germany and France) did local origination and execution. Critically, strong, trusting working relationships remained intact. As discussed in chapter 1, from my perspective, this relationship dimension is the ultimate indicator of success. I just wasn't mature enough to realise it at the time.

Through reflection, I learned the real reasons behind their reluctance. In the moment, I hadn't been aware of them, hadn't looked for them and, inexcusably, I hadn't even considered them. There were many:

- Previous centralised marketing activities — for Reebok and for direct competitors — had failed miserably. The one-size-fits-all approach had clearly not worked. These were painful and fresh memories that were difficult to erase.

- At least two of the marketing directors had been given clear directives from their bosses that under no circumstances were they to give up local advertising copy origination. I later found out that prior to our meeting, one market had already produced local copy that had been approved by his leadership team.

- Another three markets had existing media contracts in place that would need to be broken if centralisation proceeded. This would be costly and would affect partnerships that had existed for multiple years. Over a few drinks during local market visits, I also discovered that two of the newer marketing directors had joined the business primarily on the promise of being able to make their own advertising. For some, this was clearly personal.

- For a few others, it was the annoying 'not invented here' syndrome, which still to this day I cannot and will not accept.

My main reflection?

Neither party was right or wrong, and no solution was correct or incorrect. We just had different agendas. Everyone agreed that centralisation was the best thing for Europe in totality. The issue was that, at an individual market level, some units would be sacrificed. My proposal provided no relief for this detrimental impact. A harsh lesson but, in many ways, an obvious one. Fortunately, through some clear messaging by Jean Jacques and others, I compromised early and, importantly, I built trust and respect for ongoing interactions. It was an invaluable and critical insight.

Since that early experience, I have completely changed my views on what it means to be right or wrong. In essence, it simply does not matter. What matters to me is the following. That:

- I reach an outcome that is mutually agreeable to both myself and the other party that I am engaging with

- my positive working relationship with that party remains intact and, ideally, is strengthened as a result of our interaction

- I do not take a position that will compromise my values of trust and respect

- I determine the success of a relationship not by the incident or interaction itself, but rather by the enduring partnership that has hopefully been fostered.

If this means that I compromise my original position to achieve those outcomes, so be it. It also means that at times I will give up on my position completely. Even if I view that position to be 100 per cent right. It's not always right to be right.

Aside

I mentioned earlier about my regional gig having decision-making rights over the local markets. I also mentioned my strong reluctance to use them.

The former president of Reebok Europe & International, my mentor and a great friend, Roger, made a point to a group of senior execs that I have never forgotten. Reebok had recently signed a sponsorship deal with Liverpool football club. At the time, it was one of the largest commercial deals in global sports history, and definitely a massive agreement for both sides.

Like many agreements of scale, there are always teething points. At one point, a couple of the Reebok crew were flicking through the contract pages referencing a number of specific sub-clauses that were clearly not being adhered to. I recall being in the meeting when words of wisdom were shared: 'The day that you pull out a contract in front of the other party is the day that you know your relationship is over'.

Roger was an exceptional leader who was strategic, inspiring, personable, understated and oozed class. He had a knack of allowing others to take the limelight ahead of himself. Qualities I desperately try to emulate (with limited success as compared to the big man himself).

On this occasion, every one of us in the room got his message. I think he said it three times and looked every one of us directly in the eyes to ensure it got through. It did. Roger knew the value of choosing your battles. As a result, small compromises led to an enduring and tremendously beneficial partnership for both parties.

Do your best to adhere to this philosophy and coach those around you. To pull out a contractual agreement — or even reference it — must be viewed as a last resort only. If it does happen, know that the person or company on the other side of that contract will be looking closely at the early exit clause. And, even if they don't exit quickly, from that day forth, you'll never get the best from them. Human Psyche 101. It's not always right to be right.

EXCEPTIONS TO EVERY RULE

Question: will there be exceptions?

Yes, but hopefully they will be few and far between. The first is if a personal value is crossed. If it is, I will not compromise under any circumstance. I feel most people are like this. Second, if the criticality of an outcome is so important, then at times compromise will not be possible and the decision-making hierarchy will need to be followed. These instances should be by exception only.

On a final note, please be aware that this premise of 'allowable and needed compromise' relates across all business and personal interactions. It's never easy, yet always important.

Good luck. And to that certain Frenchman, Jean Jacques — merci mon ami. J'apprécie beaucoup cela.

THE PRACTICAL PART

Dealing with 'not always right to be right'

The first thing to remember is that this is not a chapter on negotiation skills or the tactics of contract engagement. This is a chapter focused on the importance of relationships and, critically, how to maintain and enhance them. I am also not suggesting that you roll over and walk away from your original stated position. Not at all. I am, however recommending that you change your tack. When you find yourself diametrically opposed from another party, consider referencing this framework (see figure 5.1).

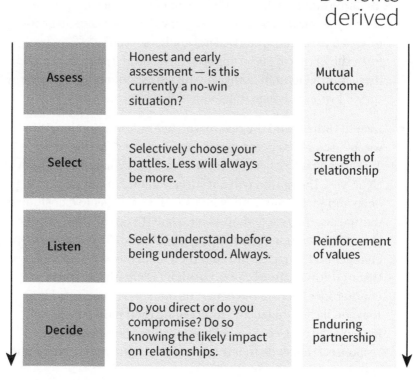

Figure 5.1: **right or wrong — a framework of compromise and hope**

- **Assess:** Quickly determine if you are in a 'no-win' situation — in other words, a situation where regardless of debate or dialogue, opposing views are too far apart to secure an aligned mutual outcome. Many times, it will be crystal clear.

- **Select:** Choose your battles carefully. Let those of low or average importance go through to the keeper. Accept them for what they are, walk away and move on. A good analogy is when people talk about the volume of 'no's' that one gives. The more 'no's' that are given, the more powerful the infrequent 'yes'.

  Being selective with your battles may sound easy. It is not. Some leaders refuse to give an inch on virtually all issues. Senior leaders can be the worst offenders because of the hierarchy of decision making that exists in most organisations. As a leader, it's important to remember that when little or no compromise is shown, people and teams below you will disengage and become resigned to inertia. They will not challenge your views or bring forth subjective or 50/50 opportunities. From their perspective, there is little point in doing so. And why should they? They know they'll lose any debate that follows. Sad but true.

- **Listen:** Understand the real reason behind the rejection. Why are we so disconnected and clearly so misaligned on this topic? There is always a reason behind a 'no' when you think it's such a clear 'yes'. The reason will not surface alone, so you need to dig deep and seek it out. Until you do, you'll never get to a position of mutual acceptance or mutual outcome. To do this, you should 'seek to understand before being understood'. This is a game changer and I suggest you commit it to memory. It also means that in the majority of cases, you don't immediately throw a counteroffer back on the table. The other party needs to know that you have listened and understood their pain points and have placed real, considered thought into your alternate response. (I concede that this last point is very much 'negotiation training 101'. Apologies!)

- **Decide:** Make the hard decision. Is it worth compromising on my original position in order to maintain the relationship, or do I play hardball and accept that the relationship will decline? To me, if you want an enduring mutual relationship, hardball should be by exception only. If you compromise, you may feel you have lost the game, but you will definitely have saved the set. Your call.

THE CRITIQUE

A brief review from Fiona Dawson, Global President, Mars Food, Multisales and Global Customers and Chair of the British Women's Business Council.

'It's not always right to be right' is a powerful lesson in life, and one that so many of us have had to learn the hard way.

As ambitious people who like winning, it can feel incredibly deflating when your ideas are not accepted, or, indeed, your decisions are wrong. As Hamish writes, it can feel incredibly personal and easy to feel under attack.

I firmly agree that when you are challenged it is vital to select your battles, and, once you have done so, you have to be prepared to listen.

Listening is perhaps one of the trickier aspects of conflict management. It's all too easy to go into 'sell' mode (or, as a coach once said to me, 'Fiona, you're just in transmit mode, not receive mode!'). The power of active listening is liberating. Not only do you understand where people are coming from, you also open yourself up to new ideas. It also allows you to be hard on the problem but soft on the person, acknowledging that you have understood their perspective and replaying what you have heard.

Over the last 32 years in business I have learnt that life is not black or white — and often it's the grey zone in between that's the most interesting, creative space where constructive conflict thrives and creativity can flourish. I have also experienced that my greatest learnings have come from some of the most difficult times.

It's impossible to be right all of the time. If you are, then you're guilty of not taking enough risks. As you navigate through issues, it is so important that you create a safe environment in your team for conflict. You must surround yourself with good people, who have shared values but diverse views, and who are prepared to put contrarian thoughts on the table. It takes courage and needs vulnerability, but the results are rewarding.

It's not about you being right, it is about doing the right thing — even if it's not easy.

Chapter 6

Noticed, Remembered, Understood

When Venus Williams burst onto the world scene, Reebok was one of the very first to snap her up. A marketeer's dream, she was the epitome of modern youth: talented, driven, stylish and generationally relevant. An exceptional athlete and an exceptional signing.

I recall one of our research agencies developing a new tracking methodology. They labelled it 'The Cool List'. It measured who was cool. How cool were they? How long had they been cool? What stage of cool were they? Who thought they were cool? What could keep them cool?

The cool list was endless.

Most organisations do the same. For their brands and for their corporate reputation, they spend a fortune on building and measuring brand equity. Yet ironically, for our number one asset — ourselves — we do stuff-all.

Pretty uncool, I reckon.

THE MESSAGE ··························

I have always marvelled at outstanding marketing. The ability of brands to consistently reinvent themselves and remain generationally relevant is an art form to behold. This chapter attempts to replicate that. Not in a traditional advertising sense, but applied to the most important asset we have in the world: ourselves. I appreciate this may sound a little selfish. Maybe it is, but is it necessarily a bad thing? When we are progressing, developing and advancing as an individual we are hard to beat. And when we are at our very best, the companies we are part of will always benefit.

Be aware that I'm not talking about standard self-development. Other chapters and a plethora of books go into that. What I'm talking about is the ability to market and promote yourself like an outstanding piece of advertising. If you have worked on, been exposed to, or led a marketing campaign of significance, you will know the effort, diligence and carefully plotted professionalism that goes into making it a resounding success. Despite perception, luck is seldom involved and hard work is mandatory.

Wouldn't it be great to scaffold your own career and personal growth story on such a tried and tested model? I think so, and I don't think it's that hard to achieve. You just need to transform yourself into the greatest piece of creative advertising ever produced.

··························

Of all my practical learnings over the years, 'Noticed, Remembered, Understood' is one of the best. It pertains to what exceptional advertising looks like. Stay with me, as I promise there is a relevant link beyond marketing puffery.

THREE STEPS TO EXCEPTIONAL

There are numerous analytical scorecards that define what makes great advertising copy. I have lived and breathed many of these, from my very first days in the London advertising industry to the multimillion-dollar production budgets of the global sports world through to the meticulous attention to detail of calculating 'return on investment' expenditure within the consumer goods market.

Each scorecard has its own merits and every year there will be an improvement on how best to measure advertising success. All that said, three simple words remain the easiest way for me to describe what great advertising looks like:

1. Noticed

2. Remembered

3. Understood.

If you nail these three elements, in that order, you will be well versed in communications success.

Credit for these words, and the process of measuring them, belong completely to Professor Bruce McColl (former Mars Global Chief Marketing Officer) and Dr Byron Sharp (Ehrenberg-Bass Institute), both also mentioned in chapter 4. I am not going to detail what they mean in an advertising sense — that's for another book, and definitely one not written by me.

What I will tell you is how I have used these words for building personal leadership brands, across all levels of an organisation. They assist not only with personal growth, but equally with career development and progression. If you can master them, like a great piece of advertising, positive conversations will begin.

Intrigued? Read on.

A lot of successful people have spoken at length about how difficult it is to break through the clutter that exists in modern corporate life. Many say it's harder to stand out today than it was yesterday. Unsurprisingly, most who say this are old. (I may be ageing, but I hope I am not one of them.)

I think it's the opposite: the ability for one to stand tall and play large within a business sense has never been greater.

'Old school' business and social constructs are being eradicated. Organisational hierarchy has flattened, and corporate bureaucracy is viewed as dated, inefficient and irrelevant. Egalitarian work practices where everyone's opinions count are now commonplace. And when you see senior partners from the 'Big Four' accounting firms sitting next to new starters in an open-plan office, you know change is upon us.

Interaction between senior leaders and employees at all levels is now a regular occurrence. Board members, CEOs and functional directors are mentoring and coaching new starters, apprentices and graduates. Reverse mentoring, to keep leaders generationally relevant, is now prominent in most leading organisations, and visible leadership through digital forums is now routine. Interacting with the heads of billion-dollar global corporations, once an impossibility, is now reality.

The forums for exposure and interaction are definitely available. The question therefore, is how *does* one break through?

NOTICED

At university, I had a mate who was doing a similar marketing and business degree to myself. Like many of us, he desperately wanted to get into the world of advertising. It so happens, he was more desperate than most. Yet after sending dozens of CVs to every advertising agency in New Zealand and Australia, he had received no response. Not even one official rejection letter. Considering his qualifications were considerably better than those of his cohort, mild despair simmered among us all.

One thing about Mike, though, was that he was a tenacious and determined bugger. He decided to take things into his own hands. He attached his CV to a large red brick and hurled it through the window of one of Wellington's pre-eminent advertising agencies.

Needless to say, he got noticed. Unfortunately, it was not by the agency — just the police and local court authorities.

Back to today. The first rule of breaking through the clutter is to get noticed. It's the same rule for all levels of seniority. It doesn't matter what you say, what you deliver or what you stand for unless you can get noticed. So many gifted people have failed at this very first stage, when what they have to offer is sometimes exceptional. To me, this is a massive lost opportunity for everyone.

In an advertising sense, unless you are noticed within the first few seconds of delivery (especially on digital platforms), everything else that follows is totally redundant.

Does this mean you have to be exceptionally bold and loud in everything that you do? Do you have to be the extrovert with boundless charisma? The controversial provocateur? Or even the 'out-there' Kiwi brick-thrower I mentioned earlier?

I don't think so. For some, however, it will mean stepping outside of your comfort zone. This could mean putting your hand up for projects that are foreign to your competency set. It may involve bringing an external perspective into the organisation that is new, challenging and provocative. Or, you may simply decide to be the one who gives their honest opinion on a mission-critical subject. Either way, your methods do not have to be overtly clever. Or borderline criminal!

Aside

Everyone has their own opinion on what makes the best type of leader. The leaders that I admire tend to be unassuming. They lead by example. They are modest and humble, and they promote others ahead of themselves. They listen, are open to challenge, willing to change, and, where necessary, do change.

One of my favourite Māori proverbs is 'Kāore te kumara e kōrero mō tōna ake reka': 'the kumara (sweet potato) does not say how sweet he is'. I like this.

It's also worth noting that great leaders do not have to be the most charismatic or extroverted people going. While charisma is clearly a benefit, if you don't have it in spades, don't use it as an excuse not to be noticed. Business and society require diverse leaders, including the quiet ones.

And if you are quiet, there's research to make you feel better. The Henley Business School believes that neither introverts nor extroverts make the best leaders: the most effective leadership requires a balance of the two. They also have anecdotal evidence that suggests it is significantly easier to teach an introvert how to communicate more assertively than it is to teach an extrovert how to be a more considerate listener. Makes sense.

REMEMBERED

In advertising, this relates to brand recognition. Once your audience has sat up and noticed the message, the next job is to ensure that they know what brand it is for. This means consistently building and leveraging a brand's distinctive assets, including logos, shapes, colours and claims and, where beneficial, using 'borrowed memory structures' to aid recognition. (Essentially communicating these assets on a regular basis and doing so in a consistent manner.)

We can take this ethos and apply it directly to our own personal leadership brand. Each of us will have distinctive assets that are unique, easily identifiable and instantly recognised by others. Just like a brand, we will have some assets that are firmly entrenched while others will need refinement or possibly even creation. I term these assets your 'signature processes'. They demand consistency in execution and maximum leverage.

At the end of this chapter, I provide a framework for developing your personal leadership brand. Signature processes are a key component, and I've provided a few of the more notable examples I've come across in my career.

A word of advice

Presentation skills matter.

Many try to push them aside, yet their importance for business success is obvious. Conversely, if they are a weakness, it can be a potential career staller. Although there are many speech training courses available, the best breakthroughs I have seen are when I send individuals or teams to theatre workshops or drama classes. These definitely push them out of their comfort zone, yet on every occasion—and across three continents now—it has worked a treat.

UNDERSTOOD

Being noticed and remembered is not enough; you need to be understood. Within advertising, it means people understand and resonate with the message that your brand is communicating. Flashy and dazzling spots that cut through and have instant brand recognition are lost if people do not comprehend their message or cannot relate to them. It's the same with your personal leadership brand.

Being understood in a leadership sense means that the values and messages that you portray are fully comprehended by others. This also means that they are aligned with the organisation that you work for. If they are misaligned, your messaging is likely to confuse your audience and your personal brand will not resonate. The best way to be understood is a two-fold approach. Always start with communicating why this issue or topic is so important to you and the organisation. Never hide from this. And second, keep your language as simple as possible — clear, concise and understandable. Jargon for the sake of it is not only overrated, it's often dangerously confusing.

Be aware, leaders also have to deliver messages that are not always welcome. It is one of the difficult and challenging parts of leadership. If you deliver tough messages in a manner that is consistent with your values (and those of the company), regardless if others agree with your messages or not, they will at least understand them and where you are coming from.

To me, this is the ultimate in authenticity. Crack this one, and you're doing well.

THE PRACTICAL PART

Your personal leadership brand

There are literally hundreds of different models to define what a brand stands for. These include brand pyramids, brand DNAs and brand scores.

Unfortunately, I am yet to discover a great personal leadership brand template that has universal application. If you have one, I suggest you publish it quickly. In its absence, I have developed the following framework (see figure 6.1). It may look complex and cumbersome, yet it is easy to complete and has made considerable difference to those who have used it.

Where to start:

- **Leadership purpose:** State what your true purpose of leadership is. What do you get out of bed for every morning and strive to do as a leader and server of others? One sentence, maximum.

- **Passion/values and talents:** This sounds easy to do. It is not. Prior to listing, refer to chapter 18, Who is writing your agenda?, for a detailed explanation on what they mean and how best to identify them.

- **Energy drivers:** Define what they are for you. Conversely, what are those things that drain the energy from you? Your objective is to do more that drives your energy and avoid the things that drain you like the plague.

- **Leadership competencies:** Define the core leadership traits that you want to be known for. In marketing, some people refer to this as 'brand fame'. In this case, what do you personally want to be famous for from a leadership perspective?

Personal Leadership Brand

_____

(My leadership purpose)

My leadership competencies	My functional competencies
1 _____	1 _____
2 _____	2 _____
3 _____	3 _____
4 _____	4 _____

My passions and values	My talents
1 _____	1 _____
2 _____	2 _____
3 _____	3 _____
4 _____	4 _____

My energy drivers

Radiators	_Drains_
1 _____	1 _____
2 _____	2 _____
3 _____	3 _____
4 _____	4 _____

My signature processes/artifacts

_____   _____

_____   _____

Figure 6.1: personal leadership brand model

- **Functional competencies:** Define the core functional attributes that define you as a leader. Even if you are a CEO or generalist, we still need functional and foundational capabilities of note. Without these competencies, we would simply be masters of mediocrity. For reference, Facebook head office has a rule that all leaders continue functional capability building throughout their career. It's a different approach, and I like it.

- **Signature processes:** Decide what they are for you. Then, just like a distinctive asset for a brand, consistently improve, leverage and monitor progress. Some of my own signature processes are as follows:

  — **My annual New Year's letter:** for 19 consecutive years, I have written a personal and informal letter to each of my direct reports. I'm not sure who I feel most sorry for: those who have to read them or Maddie and the kids, who have to put up with me taking three days every Christmas holiday to write them.

    Business is always secondary. I start with a mindset of 'If I was in your shoes, I would do the following'. I have written about issues of health, attitude and personal growth. At times, I have recommended that people leave the business and, where needed, leave their current leader — meaning myself.

    To date, I have not had any official complaints to the HR department. Not that I am aware of anyway! My teams, and indeed many others, know me for these letters and I attribute them as a definite signature process.

  — **Personal notes:** the day I joined the Wrigley company, I received a handwritten note (scanned via email) from the Global Head of Strategy. He was a senior member of Bill Wrigley's Chicago-based leadership team. The message was one of congratulations on my appointment and a welcome to the family. I still have this note from Peter.

I have stolen this idea with pride. Almost to a fault, every new starter within a business under my remit — and often, those beyond — will receive a similar type of personal note. Additionally, I acknowledge promotions, birthdays and extraordinary efforts or results with similar handwritten notes. It must drive my PAs crazy at times to manage all of these.

Coupled with this, I am known for writing small, often annoying, notes on small pieces of paper during meetings. New ideas, requests and inspirations are passed daily to relevant attendees. Worse still, models are often sketched on napkins (a habit originating from my boozy lunch days in London advertising). I feel sorry for the recipients of these notes — regardless of the content, my handwriting is shocking.

— **Authentic storytelling:** I never used to do this. A good friend of mine, an exceptional leader and one of the best mentors I have experienced, pulled me aside many years ago. We were in Munich and I had just done a presentation to the European confections team. His message: 'You are a good presenter, yet you would be so much better if you told authentic personal stories. Let people know why you value the requests and demands you are making of them. Make it personal and it will resonate'.

I followed Juan's advice immediately, yet the reason I did it was purely results oriented. I did it manipulatively to make me more effective, and it took me a good 12 months to realise my failing. Yes, Juan's advice provided better results, but, more importantly, I came to realise it was just the right thing to do. Explaining the reason behind why one feels so passionate about a particular topic or request is not just about chasing a result; it's about being totally authentic.

Nowadays, I like to think most people remember and identify authenticity within me. It's an important part of my leadership brand.

— **Constantly dissatisfied and wanting new:** This is a strange one to classify as a distinctive signature process, yet I believe it holds true. To a fault, those who know me understand that I'm never satisfied with the current position and status quo. I am always wanting more, seeking new, searching for different and striving for next. Drives a lot of people nuts, yet it is ingrained within me.

Aside

Everyone is different, which makes life and leaders fascinating. I have experienced leaders who have signature processes that are unique and distinctly recognisable to them alone. They include:

- having a drum kit in their office and regularly jamming out a beat during morning and afternoon meetings

- conducting 'one on one' meetings with their direct reports while road cycling in Lycra

- taking daily phone calls while on a treadmill or rower

- only accepting phone calls or in-person communication and refusing to open, let alone reply to, any emails

- meditating daily in a doorless glass-walled office

- opening every presentation with a quote and finishing every presentation with a rhetorical question

- having an annoyingly loud yet infectious laugh

- wearing outlandishly colourful trousers every single day of his career — legendary, Denis!

MODELS FOR THE WHITEBOARD

Tracking Your Signature Processes

The model shown in figure 6.2 was developed by Professor Jenni Romaniuk of the Ehrenberg-Bass Institute.

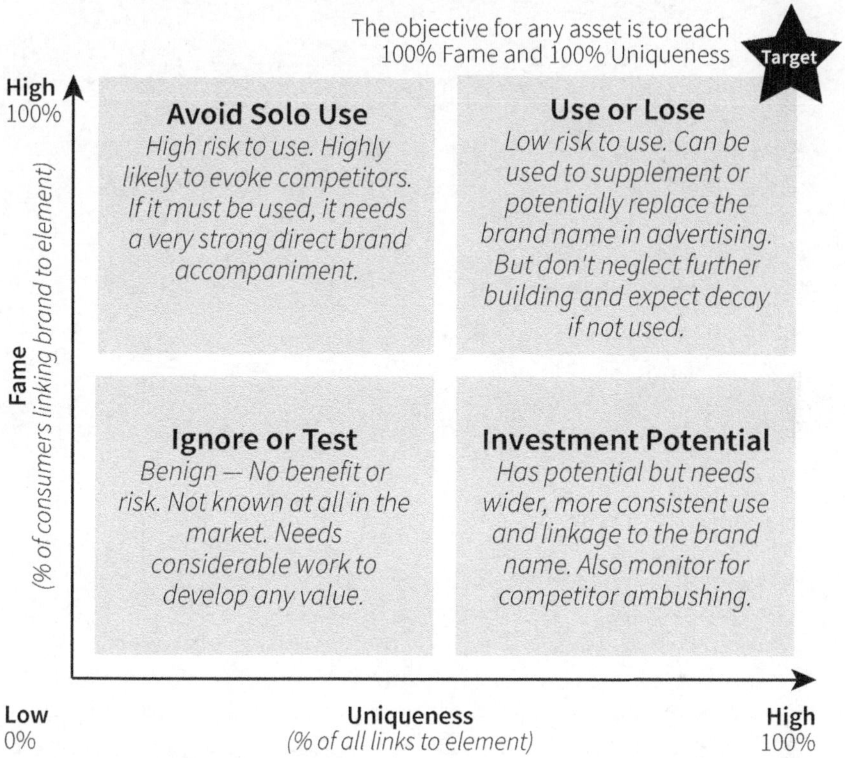

The objective for any asset is to reach 100% Fame and 100% Uniqueness **Target**

Fame
(% of consumers linking brand to element)

High
100%

Avoid Solo Use
High risk to use. Highly likely to evoke competitors. If it must be used, it needs a very strong direct brand accompaniment.

Use or Lose
Low risk to use. Can be used to supplement or potentially replace the brand name in advertising. But don't neglect further building and expect decay if not used.

Ignore or Test
Benign — No benefit or risk. Not known at all in the market. Needs considerable work to develop any value.

Investment Potential
Has potential but needs wider, more consistent use and linkage to the brand name. Also monitor for competitor ambushing.

Low
0%

Uniqueness
(% of all links to element)

High
100%

Figure 6.2: your signature processes

It relates directly to a brand's distinctive assets; however, I have equally used it for positioning and developing one's own personal leadership assets and qualities — that is, your signature processes. Even if you do not have quantifiable data to help you complete the model, seek open feedback from others to give you a sense of where you currently sit and set a path of action going forward to create your ideal end state. It's a very powerful tool. Thank you, Jenni.

THE CRITIQUE

A brief review from Julien Lemoine, Managing Director & VP CLM BBDO, Paris, and Global Advertising Account Lead for Mars/Wrigley.

I wholeheartedly agree with Hamish, but I will always take the opportunity to push a client a bit more.

Hamish talks about the 'ability to market and promote yourself like an outstanding piece of advertising'. My push would be do it authentically. It's not about 'creating your own brand'. It's about starting with the real you. Embrace who you really are and what makes you different — whatever that is. The most memorable pieces of advertising are authentic.

By starting from something that is genuinely you, you won't have to make much effort to shine (i.e. get Noticed), so you'll do it consistently better. And as this comes from your true self, people will easily associate it with you (i.e. it will be Remembered). My unruly curly hair became my own distinctive asset for years. (But now that I'm losing it, I probably need to figure out the next thing. A word of advice: pick something that lasts!)

A recent article on the Snickers chocolate bar's 'you're not you' campaign, one that is close to the heart for my agency and one I had the honour to work on, talks about how BBDO orchestrated for Mars the most successful comeback of the decade. This success was down to one thing: making the conscious decision to obey the first rule of branding. If people are going to remember my brand, first they must know it is me (meaning consistent and repeatable storytelling of what the brand stands for).

Hamish also mentions the need to go outside of one's comfort zone to be noticed. Going outside of your comfort zone is important to grow yourself, discover new versions of you, but not truly to be noticed. Some of the most noticeable people can be the most awkward introverts. You can be noticed for anything, and sometimes just being different and comfortable with it can work for you. Embrace your own difference.

By being genuine you'll be Noticed and Remembered. Sure, you won't always be for everyone, but faking another personality is too hard and would lead you to attract the wrong people — you would likely be misunderstood.

'Understood' is the least sexy, but critical for effective leadership. We spend a lot of time thinking about what we are going to say and how we will say it, the story around it, but we often forget to ask ourselves how this message will be heard. Leave a tiny space of ambiguity and people will surely misinterpret it. But if you have empathy for your audience and you think through how your message will be heard by them, you will be understood and your authenticity comes through in spades.

Bringing it all together requires accepting your own vulnerability. Vulnerability is usually a package deal to be Noticed, Remembered and Understood all at once. Humans are naturally drawn to raw, unfiltered emotions. Emotions are how we connect, and leadership is about connecting. I still remember one of the Mars segment presidents letting his tears run in a speech he was making in front of all his key top 100 leaders. Trust me when I say this was noticed and remembered. Showing vulnerability means people inevitably hear the truth. No ambiguity (so it's Understood).

So, I would rephrase Hamish to 'Embody and promote your own true brand as the outstanding piece of creative you are'.

Chapter 7

Ever **Heard** of **Harry** Redknapp?

A few years back, I shared the following Mark Twain quote with my three kids and not one of them got it: 'When I was a boy of 14, my father was so ignorant I could hardly stand to have the old man around. But when I got to be 21, I was astonished at how much he had learned in seven years'. Their response was, 'Yep, pretty clear that old man needed to grow up'. Classic. A few years on, I would be curious to see if they had a different answer. If it remains the same, I'll need to rewrite this chapter.

Experience really is a fascinating phenomenon: invaluable, yet underleveraged.

If only we could appreciate experience when insight takes place, in those moments of anguish, occasions of discovery and instants of reflection. They add belief, reassurance and confidence, which are all beneficial for those we serve.

Now, that would be special.

THE MESSAGE ························

'If I knew then what I know now, how success would be mine.' So very true. I love the value of experience; it has definitely made me that much better. Not just in a business sense, but also as a partner, parent and hopefully as a friend. When I say better, I am talking of being more productive and more efficient. A better decision maker and a better leader. I am more supportive and more challenging, an improved delegator and an increased provider of freedom and autonomy. I have enhanced my care and empathy for others, alongside my desire for 'doing good' for others. This comes with having a better mindset and a better sense of self-worth.

Things that used to worry me now seldom get attention. If they do, they're handled with perspective, hopefully poise and with a deeper sense of confidence.

Over time, I believe most people are like this. Understandably so: we take experiences from our past and, in the majority of cases, we use insight and learning to enable us to be that much better next time around. If only we could garner those insights earlier in our career — indeed, earlier in our life.

I would like to add one more thing. Speaking from experience, we shouldn't get too worried about getting old. As a certain football manager will tell us, so long as we remain passionate, we will always be better.

···

A chapter on experience: a topic I'm passionate about, and one that falls short of the attention and credit it so richly deserves.

Allow me to start with benefits of experience. Following every major issue, incident or opportunity that I have experienced, I have developed, grown and improved as a leader and as a person. Like many of the concepts I discuss in this book, my development was not instantaneous, but it was always forthcoming. For me, experience has provided the following benefits and, when collectively combined, each is greater than their individual worth.

THE ABILITY TO MANAGE AND NEGOTIATE EMOTION

Situations and scenarios that once would send me into a panic now elicit a different (and improved) approach. With the perspective that comes from experience, where once I'd be stressed, now I'm calm. Where once I'd be emotional, I now am considered. Where once I'd be angered, now I'm composed. All improvements based on experience. Richard Branson once described business as being like an emotional rollercoaster: 'There will be fantastic moments when you are soaring and feel untouchable, and others where you plunge into chaos and all you can do is try to hold on'. From my perspective, what makes you 'hold on' is the knowledge and experience that despair is temporary and that those exceptional moments are just around the corner.

THE ABILITY TO LEARN THROUGH ADVERSITY

This is a truism that drives my frustration levels through the roof. In chapter 16, Constant dissatisfaction, I talk about how I have an insatiable desire to get ahead of the curve. This means to:

- lead versus manage

- shape versus react

- show versus tell

- fix before breaking.

I love these concepts and I strive to do them daily. Yet, in reality, I fail miserably. Fortunately, I am in good company.

Steve Hansen, the former All Blacks Rugby World Cup–winning coach, has said, 'You don't need to lose to learn. But it sure helps.' Although every learning experience has its advantages, without a doubt the biggest lessons come as a result of failure or adversity. When things go against plan, we think, we analyse and we scrutinise to unimaginable levels. It is human nature, and as long as we learn from these painful moments, we will perpetually improve. Experience makes these painful moments less dramatic and less hurtful. We know they have a silver lining, and history tells us we will be better as a result of them.

THE ABILITY TO LEARN THROUGH OTHERS

Sometimes the best lessons in life occur in a room other than your own. They are lessons derived from others who are often separate from your circle of influence, outside your area of expertise and detached from your inner perspective. When you are emotionally removed from a situation and its inevitable baggage, you can reflect with objectivity. I often remind myself that experience is not always derived from tenure or age: it can be moment specific, incident specific and even culturally specific. Effective leadership is about insatiable curiosity and the ability to seamlessly connect disconnected occurrences. Learning through others is a brilliant example of this.

Aside

Here's a good example of learning through others.

Every three years, I do my standard round of connecting with executive search firms. Executive search firms are recruiters who generally deal with senior-level corporate appointments and are habitual providers of very sound career advice. During one of these interactions, we got onto the topic of my eventual retirement and what would be next following a life of corporate experience. Very casually, I mentioned that maybe when I hit my mid fifties I would likely step away from the big bad corporate world, relax a bit and do something completely different. Now, I still have a few years to go before I get to my mid fifties, so I thought it was quite a harmless comment. Big lesson learned: never say this to a senior recruiter.

For the next 30 minutes, I was told in no uncertain terms how crazy and wrong this would be. The gist of it was: 'Why would you even contemplate stepping away at that age? That's the time you'd be at your very best.

You'd be at the height of your capabilities, and, with the experiences you would've had, you'd be more valued than ever. Plus, that's usually the age when senior leaders enjoy themselves the most: they're more composed, more curious and working for the right reasons. You'll be financially secure, so you won't be reliant on your job, so you won't be in "prove" mode, and you'll be making the right decisions not because of others, but because you believe they're the right ones to make. You'd be crazy to retire at that age. Experience should never be undervalued. Never'.

Two lessons learned: do not underestimate the importance of experience, and never casually mention early retirement to a recruiter. Even if you want to learn how to fly fish.

THE ABILITY TO LEARN THROUGH IMMERSION

I like immersion due to its practicality. Unquestionably, you learn by doing and there is no better way to gain insight than by getting your hands dirty. You immediately gain an appreciation and a realisation of specific situations. Previous vague political statements are replaced with considered, pragmatic and substantiated declarations of direction. Compelling future visions are now supported with believable rationale, realistic processes and clear steps for implementation. After you've been immersed, there is no need for unsubstantiated claims. Moreover, absorption can lead to transformation. A strong grounding of knowledge provides the foundation for creativity and innovation. Although we are led to believe that leadership is 'blue sky, helicopter view' management, in my mind it is anything but.

Poor leaders believe they know, average leaders observe to understand, while exceptional leaders immerse to break through.

THE ABILITY TO LEARN THROUGH SELF

I find this one difficult to describe, and maybe description isn't even necessary. I'm talking about the continual observation, reflection and refinement of one's self. It happens naturally and often automatically. Over time and with experience, we apprehend what makes us tick. We understand our moral compass, our passions, strengths and indeed weaknesses. What was once all encompassing is now insignificant in context. In essence, through experience, we know ourselves better today than we did yesterday.

Aside

You may have noticed that I have not mentioned 'the ability to learn through success'. It's not an oversight. I highlight its importance in chapter 9, The 3 A's (and one critical E) where I talk about the concept of 'appreciative enquiry' and the benefits of positive reflection. It's a powerful tool to ensure repeated success and, above all, brilliantly practical.

BELIEVE IN EXPERIENCE

Why do some of us rarely understand, recognise or appreciate the true value of experience? Mark Twain gives kids an out when it comes to understanding, yet, for me, even in my late thirties, I was a massive doubter. I used to regularly ask myself what experience is really worth. One hypothesis I had for feeling like this, was an inherent belief that I alone, a person who had been promoted into positions of responsibility at a reasonably early age, had to have all the answers. I viewed it as my responsibility — it was almost unacceptable not to have the solution at hand.

So, in the absence of firm knowledge, I started reading. Scientific and psychological journals related specifically to the topic of experience started to pile up on my desk. Serotonin and brain regeneration articles were spread across the kitchen table. Cerebrum, neurons and axons were casually raised over dinner conversations and mornings at our house saw philosophical debates on the 'experiencing self' versus the' 'remembering self'.

Aside

Nobel Prize winner and behavioural economics researcher Daniel Kahneman talks about these concepts. In his book *Thinking, Fast and Slow*, he describes the Experiencing Self as one that experiences the emotion of the moment, while the Remembering Self is the memory of the experienced moment.

He uses the example of someone listening to a symphony and hearing 20 minutes of glorious music. At the very end of the performance, there are a dreadful few seconds of screeching sounds. The Remembering Self will believe that the entire experience was ruined. This is the negative memory they will keep. When in fact the Experiencing Self had 20 minutes of delight. But because of those last few seconds, that delight counts for nothing to the Remembering Self.

I often remind my marketing, sales and corporate affairs teams of the Experiencing Self versus the Remembering Self. I have them focus on the very last messages that are left with consumers, customers and stakeholders. We all know the importance of 'opening hooks', yet few focus on the essential close.

This links perfectly to the concept of negativity bias that I discuss in chapter 8, Bad bosses are great bosses. It's important to be aware of this bias as you will have many experiences that are largely positive, yet tainted by one or two small factors. These negative factors usually occur at the very end of the experience itself. Do your best not to lose capturing positive experiences.

Back to my academic reading. It was fascinating, yet at the end of it, I had two conclusions.

The first was that I was absolutely none the wiser. The second was that Maddie had always called me borderline boring, but my latest obsession was bringing me dangerously close to 'spare room' marriage material. Let me focus on the former.

Most of what I was reading went completely over my head; not once in my quest for knowledge did I find a simple, relevant chart that linked experience to productivity. Nothing special or overtly clever was needed, just a basic quantitative correlation between the two showing that the more experience you have, the better you will be. Yet apart from hypotheticals and theory-oriented models, I could not find my desired chart. If one exists, please send it to me. In the interim though, I had an alternate source. It was called football.

INTRODUCING HARRY

Harry Redknapp is an English former football player and manager. He retired from management in late 2017, having had considerable success over many a year. Most notably an FA Cup win with Portsmouth in 2008 and overseeing the return of Tottenham Hotspur to the UEFA Champions League at the end of the 2010–11 season. These are no easy feats.

Following one particular match, Harry was asked by a journalist if he was worried about the recent introduction of so many young European football managers into the English Premier League. Harry must have been in his early sixties at the time, and these young whippersnappers were in their early forties at best. It was clear that the interviewer was trying to goad Harry into a knee-jerk response.

But Harry's answer was short and typically direct: 'No, I'm not worried. I will always be better.'

The journalist was a little perplexed. Like all annoyingly good journalists, he immediately asked a second question. It was the same as the first. Harry answered with exactly the same response. After a silence that seemed to last an eternity on live TV, Harry rescued the journalist and elaborated: 'As long as I am as passionate as the other managers, I will always be better. Better because of my experience.'

Despite being a long-suffering Arsenal fan, I completely bought into his answer.

Passion is a non-negotiable. Even if you memorise a management system that captures every historical insight of old—and current artificial intelligence (AI) systems do this, by the way—if you don't have passion, then it's game over. But, passion being equal, experience will always trump those without it.

Thank you, Harry: your insight allowed me to put the academic journals away and for the time being, the spare room remains unused.

Aside

The pace of change can be overwhelming for many. Everyone has talked of VUCA (volatility, uncertainty, complexity and ambiguity) and even Super VUCA for years now. Originally leveraged by the US Army College to describe the complexity of change since the end of the Cold War, it has become standard vernacular in every strategic planning session.

Personally, I reckon VUCA has always existed. Various TED talks and keynote speakers tell us that 'today will be the slowest pace of change that we will ever experience'. I don't disagree, but I also would say it is a tautology that existed 100 years ago and 1000 years before that. Change is inevitable and it happens constantly.

But rather than thinking too hard or too long about how to keep up and keep adapting with change, remind yourself how much more capable and more efficient you are today versus when you were younger.

LISTEN, REFINE AND GROW

Here are three seemingly small yet powerful examples of leadership change derived from experience. The first is personal, the second is strategic and the third is functional.

PERSONAL LEARNING

Sydney, Australia, 2014. I had just finished a meeting at Fox Studios. I was with a well-respected member of my leadership team — someone I classify as a good friend. Over coffee, she shared some personal challenges that she had been going through. Although it shouldn't be the case, it's difficult to show vulnerability and openness to your boss. (This is one of

It's Not Always Right to be Right

the reasons I'm a firm believer in the importance of being 'respected and liked' as a leader; I talk about this in chapter 12, What would Margaret Thatcher say?) After a few minutes of her opening up, it turned emotional. A few tears were shed.

I'm not sure why, but I have never been great in these situations. I do feel genuine compassion and empathy — a massive amount, actually, and I carry that with me for long periods. Nonetheless, I am also the typical Kiwi male who struggles in the moment to 'go there', or at the very least, to try and 'go there'.

As per standard Hamish behaviour, I expressed my sympathy and then with speed that Usain Bolt would be proud of I deflected the subject and moved on to something else. I don't recall what that 'something else' was, but I do know that it was a completely different subject, and definitely lighter in nature. (My default setting is to deflect uncomfortable situations with humour.)

What happened next was pretty special. They say feedback is a gift, and when it comes from someone you respect and like, it makes a considerable difference. What's more, when it's delivered in the moment it becomes one of the most powerful learning experiences you can encounter. Her message back to me was clear and considered, delivered with calmness and clarity: 'Hamish, when someone is clearly being so vulnerable to you, you must know, it is very important to them. Please give them the respect and the friendship to stay in the moment of pain. For as long as that moment is needed, and regardless of how uncomfortable it makes you feel.'

Of all the feedback I've had over the years — and I have had a bit — this one had the biggest impact. Just like a loss on the sporting field, the personal ones hurt the most. Consequently, they are the biggest motivators for change.

I'm still far from perfect in this domain, but I've definitely made progress. I deflect a lot less than I used to. I've realised that using deflection is a coping mechanism designed for my benefit and not that of others. I have also learned to listen more. Not respond, incessantly talk or jump immediately into solution mode. Rather, just listen. As a result, my team and personal relationships are significantly deeper.

Above all, though, I know that I would not have made progress in this area unless I went through this uncomfortable experience. One 30-minute conversation has changed and enhanced the way I interact with and lead others. I wish I had learned this earlier. This is the true power of experience. Thank you, Natalie.

STRATEGIC LEARNING

This formula (see figure 7.1) is the well-known Beckhard-Harris change equation. It is a simple way of analysing the potential success or failure of any major change initiative within a business.

$$D \times V \times F > R$$

Dissatisfaction   Vision   First steps   Resistance to change

Figure 7.1: Beckhard-Harris change equation

I don't want to talk about the model per se, but rather show you how experience has significantly changed how I use it. Let me explain:

- **Dissatisfaction (D):** No real changes, as this is me all over.

- **Vision (V):** Previously, I assumed that everyone understands the vision; if it resonated with me, it would with others. I would have talked infrequently about vision and purpose, with my main message being about strategic choice and execution. These are all schoolboy errors. Today, I attempt to make vision and purpose relevant and compelling to everyone in an organisation. If not, it will be lost and meaningless. I also measure, update and demand vision progress. Previously a desirable, it is now an essential.

- **First steps (F):** I now grasp the importance of recognising early momentum. It is infectious and a massive motivator. Previously I would have expected it, demanded it, but seldom highlighted it. Another miss.

- **Resistance to change (R):** Possibly my biggest wake-up call. I used to back myself to inspire and motivate others to change. I had false confidence that I could do this quickly and do it alone — regardless of the obstacles in front of me. Adversity and failure have since guided me to now make change momentum a clear leadership strength.

FUNCTIONAL LEARNING

This may sound department specific and a little boring; it's probably both. I literally have hundreds of these functional examples, all derived from experience.

In 2012, one of our factories in Czech Republic was experiencing a series of minor, yet frustrating, unknown quality incidents. As with every outstanding organisation, the business had an emphatic 'no excuse, no debate' mentality towards consumer quality. In fact, quality is the very first principle within Mars Incorporated and is lived and breathed by every single associate. Following many uncomfortable weeks of team analysis, all root cause outcomes were superficial at best.

My insight came through another channel — in this case, a peer. Denis was the European supply chain president and quickly steered me where I needed to go. His simple message: 'Treat every quality incident, regardless of substance or scale, with the same urgency as you would a full-fledged product recall.' This means demanding full accountability and immediacy of focus from the very first minute of discovery. You shout early and you shout loudly. To many, this may appear inconsequential. To me, it has been transformational. Despite placing additional pressure on my supply directors, my improvement and productivity in quality management alone has been significant.

THE PRACTICAL PART

How to leverage and capture the benefits of experience

This framework (see figure 7.2) illustrates how to capitalise on the many advantages of experience. The earlier you can introduce this within your career, the better.

Figure 7.2: learning from experience

- **Capture early** is critical to ensure you truly learn and benefit as quickly as possible from key experiences. When a moment of significance happens, get it down in writing. Remember, sometimes you will not appreciate the insight and learning until some weeks, months or even years later. Ensure your knowledge management system (i.e. your filing cabinet for all the good stuff) is adequate to allow consistent updates along with easy and instant accessibility. Additionally, capture positive and negative experiences. There is insight from both.

- **Seek out** challenging and 'beyond comfort zone' experiences. When senior management encounters difficult and challenging scenarios, put your hand up for leadership. Set clear success criteria to align expectations, and from day one manage the project on your own terms. The benefits of insight will be significant. But it will take confidence and curiosity to make reality.

- **Gain insight** to ensure you get optimal benefit from key experiences. Sometimes, your initial insights will be superficial or possibly even incorrect. Consider the bias of your Remembering Self versus your Experiencing Self. Where unsure, seek third-party perspective to uncover depth. Fresh eyes can be liberating.

- **Leverage and benefit** accordingly. Socialise your learning through storytelling. It's not preaching; it's transferring knowledge and insight that will benefit others. Leaders have a responsibility to do this throughout their entire career.

As you follow this framework, you'll grow in confidence. Through past experiences, particularly the painful ones, you will improve as a leader. Eventually, you'll start enjoying the journey as opposed to waiting for the destination. Most of the time, the goalposts will move by the time you're winding up to score, so it's the journey that you need to relish.

MODELS FOR THE WHITEBOARD

Functional vs Leadership Development

Over time, the best experiences to learn from will move from functional and technical to that of leadership insight. The earlier you can make this happen, the better. Many aspiring mid-level managers struggle to appreciate the criticality of leadership versus functional development. It's understandable; the majority of their results, training and experience have probably been about building technical capability. Being asked to rebalance on the less tangible and quantifiable area of leadership can be confronting, complex and often confusing.

To assist, I show the framework in figure 7.3. It's probably the simplest model in this entire book.

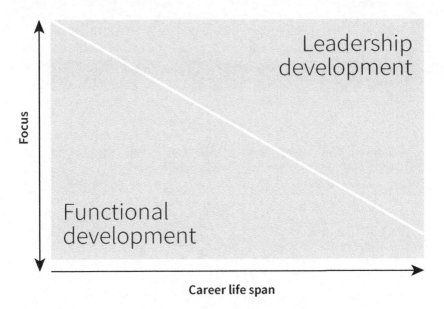

Figure 7.3: leadership vs functional development

You might also notice that the diagonal line on the model never reaches zero on functional development. My opinion differs from many on this. I believe that even the most senior leaders need to consistently work on functional development. It keeps all of us on our toes and grounded in reality.

THE CRITIQUE

A brief review from Jane Allen, Founder, Maritana Partners, Australia (a global leader and adviser in executive search for Chairs, boards and CEOs).

....

The majority of my career has been advising boards on CEO succession. To do this well, I have to ensure directors are clear on what previous experiences — both successes and challenges — will be most relevant for their next CEO to have. This includes the detailed nuances behind those experiences. As there typically isn't a perfect next leader, it is most important that a board becomes unanimously aligned behind one person.

Alignment around one person implies agreement on what experiences and knowledge will be more important than others in order to create value moving forward, while taking the least amount of risk. A candidate knowing what is perceived as important, and their ability to frame their experiences in the context of that, is often the defining factor in their success.

Although it is always a combination of skills that wins the day, people also have to be able to enjoy working together. I have seen leaders that are perfect on paper not being able to succeed if personalities can't and don't connect. You need to be able to enjoy the process of working with others, even if that takes a regular give-and-take on your part. It is far smarter to opt into a situation in which you are going to thrive than to fail when you have the experience and capability to succeed, but can't do it with those who decide whether you stay in the role or not. Best you and the client explore this fully before you commit.

One last thought.

I have noticed that, with few exceptions, the more experienced CEOs and board chairs are, the more questions they ask and the better they seem to listen to those around them.

As with the Mark Twain quote at the beginning of the chapter, the more we grow up, the more open we are to what others think and know. So, if you are in that 'master of the universe' phase of your development, use this as a warning. You may be sidelined by those open enough to continually evolve and be part of the conversation.

It is always a good idea to work hard to leverage the experiences of those around you and to be careful how and when you choose to communicate your own.

Chapter 8

Bad Bosses Are Great Bosses

I will always remember Saturday, 24 June 1995.

I was at Ellis Park, Johannesburg, South Africa, watching my beloved All Blacks lose to the Springboks in the Rugby World Cup final.

While it's still gut-wrenching, it remains etched in my memory forever not for the result, but rather for this one extraordinary man and his ability to inspire a country of 42 million people to unite as one.

Although he was not the leader on the pitch, he was clearly at the forefront of that historic victory. As he has famously said, 'Lead from the back and let others believe they are in front'.

It's a shame more of us are not like him.

THE MESSAGE ·························

Throughout your career, shit will happen. This will almost certainly include having a bad boss, or possibly even a series of bad bosses. Treat this as an opportunity and not a cause for anxiety. Relish the chance to observe them, and do so with an open mind. Document all behaviours that resonate against your values. Ingrain them in your memory and make sure you *never* repeat them as a leader.

Surprisingly, bad bosses are actually gifts. They give you the chance to learn what *not* to do. If you get landed with one, leverage the hell out of them.

It's a strange lesson, and one I did not appreciate for many years.

···

Bad bosses are actually great for one fundamental reason: the fact that we remember the painful moments more than we remember the joyful ones, which means we can really learn from them. I desperately wish it were the other way around but, unfortunately, it's not. Our minds are just not wired like that. Psychologists Paul Rozin and Edward Royzman talk about a concept called 'negativity bias'. Research shows that our brains have evolved over time to react much more strongly to negative experiences than to positive ones. Yet even in modern times, when physical danger within the corporate environment is thankfully somewhat limited, the negativity bias still exists.

Over the years I have been very fortunate to have experienced many exceptional bosses: those managers and leaders who have offered clear guidance and direction, freedom and room to stretch, development and support and, most importantly to me, respect and genuine friendship. I like to think that this has largely been down to the type of companies with which I have been associated. But with total transparency, my 'company of choice' selection at the start of my career was pure luck.

At 21, I only had one career goal: I wanted to get into the London advertising scene. I didn't care why the company existed, what they did or how they conducted themselves; I just wanted in. As luck would have it, I did get in — albeit at a very junior 'gofer' level — and landed a job within a thriving advertising agency with a great culture.

Over time I definitely became more diligent and process-oriented in company selection. Each company you work for will have its own nuances and unique idiosyncrasies, and the more laser-like you can become with your career and company selection the more it will pay dividends. The principles of those companies and individuals that I have worked with over the years have mostly been aligned and consistent with my own. As a result, I have worked with and reported to a number of very capable and exceptional leaders.

THE PERIL OF BAD BOSSES

That said, I have not been immune to the perils of bad bosses. With almost 30 years of playing this game, I have naturally had one or two. When confronted with a bad boss, you despair, you despise, you dread. Your interactions are superficial at best. Your progression and learnings are poor. Your autonomy is restricted and your freedom to operate with independence is limited. Your respect levels are downright nonexistent, and, in some cases, you fear your boss.

Worse still, which makes my blood boil, you can be harassed and bullied by your boss. In my mind, no-one has the right to believe they are better than anyone else, especially within a position of power or leadership. Yes, there will always (and should always) be an eventual hierarchy of decision making, and that is okay. But outside of that, all employees, staff, associates or whatever your organisation calls them should be treated the same. That is why some companies are exceptional and others are average, at best. My wife and I have taught our own kids to treat the Uber Eats driver with the same respect they would afford a politician or dignitary. In each case, hopefully respectfully. To me, it's just about being a good person, full stop.

Another concern is that you end up imitating the behavioural traits that you witness in a bad boss (the dreaded 'imitation factor'). If you do copy these traits, bad behaviours perpetuate widely, and you'll harm way more than just yourself. I know this is hard. Particularly if you've had little or no other experience with which to compare.

Aside

Encouragingly, a study by Shannon Taylor and Robert Folger published in the *Journal of Applied Psychology* suggests that those individuals who relied heavily on their morals and integrity to defy their manager's mistreatment or abusive approach felt strongly encouraged to prevent it from spreading further within an organisation. When offered leadership opportunities, those who have had prior experience of workplace abuse are more likely to treat their own subordinates better by learning from the bad behaviour of their bosses. Essentially, they resolve not to repeat that pattern with their own teams. It's an encouraging message for those with strong ethics and maybe gives some credence to Nietzsche's aphorism, 'What doesn't kill you makes you stronger'.

MY BAD BOSSES

If I had to categorise them, I would say that I have had three bad bosses in my career. Each of them has left me with an invaluable lesson. Lessons I did not appreciate at the time, yet lessons that helped shape an intrinsic part of my personal leadership style. Interestingly, each of them had certain qualities that were admirable — one was probably the most intellectual person that I have encountered. They were so clever that they used to confuse themselves, but that is another story. I acknowledge this because it's important to remember that everyone has admirable traits and redeemable qualities.

One of these bosses I reported to directly and the other two via indirect reporting lines. One short story is as follows. It happened many years ago now, and to date is still one of the most bewildering experiences of my career.

It was literally my second day in a new job and, for some reason unbeknown to me, I was given a couple of pieces of packaging artwork that I was told needed to be run by the head honcho.

I remember at the time thinking this was a little odd, having to show the head of a massive corporation some packaging artwork. Either way, I was working in a new industry, new company with new ways of doing things, so I casually walked over to the desk of the big man in question.

'Excuse me, I've been told that I need to show you a couple of options regarding some artwork for the upcoming promotion. Do you have a minute?'

Considering this was only my second interaction with him (the first one being at my job interview), I thought it was a reasonable opening. Without acknowledging me, he continued writing and grunted, with a slight nod of the head, something that sounded like 'whatever'.

A little perplexed, I glanced furtively around at those sitting nearby. All eyes were firmly fixed on their desks.

I continued: 'We have two options and to be honest, I don't really think there is too much difference between them. That said, I would recommend the first one based on x, y and z.'

Now, I don't remember what x, y and z were, but to this day, I insist they would have been reasonably pragmatic as I generally don't use fluff or too much marketing malarkey within my recommendations. Maybe I shouldn't have started with 'there being little difference' between the two options, but, apart from that, I reckon it wasn't a bad little 90 seconds of communication.

Well, how wrong could I be?

With one large hand he swept the artwork flying to the floor. Scraping back his chair, he stood to his full height and glared at me, almost frothing at the mouth. In a voice that I reckon half the city could hear, he let loose with, 'I want people who build brands, fucken brands! Not people who tell me what I can and can't fucken do, who the hell do you think you are ... ' Let me tell you, 30 seconds can feel like an eternity when the boss is abusing you in front of a whole office. Having exhausted his use of expletives, he pushed his chair away from his desk and trudged off, leaving me gobsmacked, humiliated and pretty upset.

I shot an incredulous look at no-one in particular and traipsed sheepishly back to my desk with one thought in my mind: 'What the hell was that all about?' Looking around the office for clarity and support from others, I realised all eyes seemed fixed on the floor. You could have heard a pin drop.

I do want to be clear that I don't base my classification of a bad boss on one or even a few isolated experiences. We all have bad days, and I am no exception. Unfortunately, in this case, this behaviour was not so isolated. It resulted in a reluctance by subordinates to interact with him and, more so, it lessened their desire to challenge or raise alternate points of view — a situation that is never good. Granted, this individual remains one of the most commercially astute and results-oriented leaders that I've met. In many areas, he was phenomenal and well respected. However, he will never make my 'exceptional leaders list'.

MY LESSONS LEARNED

First, I will always show trust, dignity and respect to all those I encounter. These were strongly held values ingrained in me from childhood. Through experiences like the one mentioned, they are now cemented. I attempt to demonstrate them privately, in one-on-one situations, and externally, whenever visible to others. Your shadow as a leader is cast far and wide; your actions and behaviours will be looked at and more than likely imitated by others. I know I have a responsibility to showcase a code of behaviour for others to emulate. This does not mean I will not show tough love or avoid crucial conversations — they are a necessity in virtually all areas of life — but, following lessons like this, I have and always will treat people with respect.

I also learned the importance of pushing back and standing up for yourself. As discussed in chapter 13, Bring on the grilling, I am a firm believer that when you deserve a dressing-down, you need to suck it up, take your medicine and learn from it. Where it is not warranted, however, I believe it is critical to push back. It's a fine line to tread and you should always be respectful when doing so.

Following this particular incident, whenever I stood up for myself — which, by the way, was on all occasions that followed — I had valuable interactions with the aforementioned manager. It worked because it showed him my conviction on a particular topic. I now know this is exactly what he wanted to see from me. Our conversations moved from diatribe to debate to value-add dialogue. It enabled me to get the very best coaching and insight from him and provided me with outstanding learning opportunities along the way.

Third, I learned that everyone, regardless of style, has valuable insights and benefits on offer. You just have to look for them. Previously, I would have viewed a bad boss as simply being a poor role model and my sole focus would have been on securing a new role, new boss and potentially new location. Since then, I now dig deep and search for insight.

I classify my final learning as a benefit, yet I am sure some coaches would tell me otherwise. Having been exposed to these types of experiences, I know I am infinitely more stoic and resilient. Today, if I do receive a 'serve of note', I often hear a little voice in the back of my mind say something like 'Is that the best you've got?' I know this is wrong and it is not the voice I should be listening to, yet it keeps on coming up! Nowadays, unless the serve hits a real personal blind spot, I don't tend to get too upset.

I am grateful to that person for showing me the way by portraying what not to do. I am definitely a better leader through these experiences.

In summary, why the heck should we value that person who is clearly a bad boss? Because they impart lasting memories, painfully ingrained into our psyches and hopefully never to be repeated. That's why.

THE PRACTICAL PART

Steps when dealing with a bad boss

Figure 8.1 is the process that I follow when dealing with a bad boss. It's simplistic, yet it has guided me and others effectively to date.

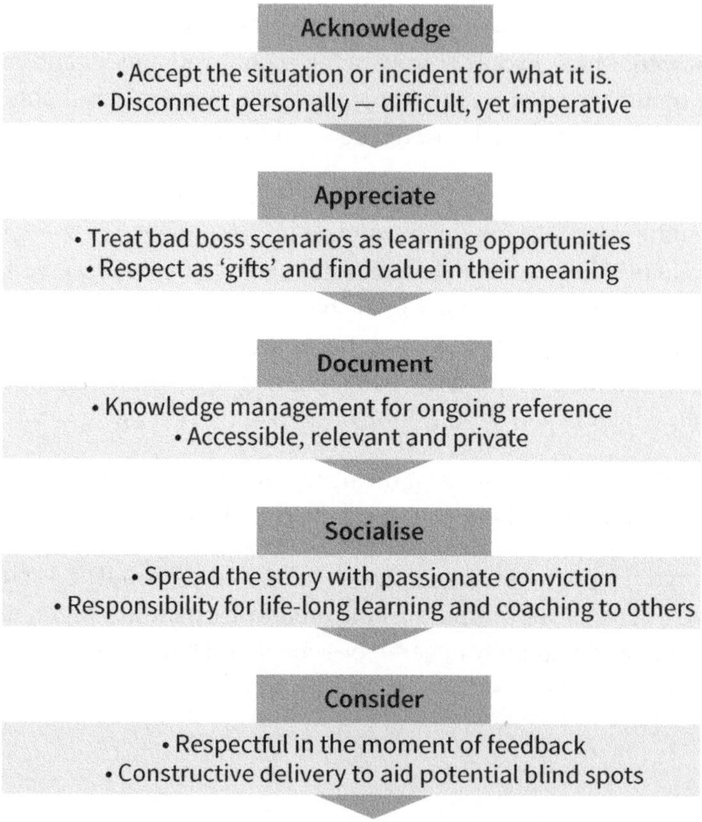

Acknowledge
- Accept the situation or incident for what it is.
- Disconnect personally — difficult, yet imperative

Appreciate
- Treat bad boss scenarios as learning opportunities
- Respect as 'gifts' and find value in their meaning

Document
- Knowledge management for ongoing reference
- Accessible, relevant and private

Socialise
- Spread the story with passionate conviction
- Responsibility for life-long learning and coaching to others

Consider
- Respectful in the moment of feedback
- Constructive delivery to aid potential blind spots

Figure 8.1: bad bosses and invaluable insights — a 5-step learning process

- **Acknowledge:** When you experience a situation or adverse behaviour from a bad boss, recognise it straight away for what it is. Nothing more, nothing less. Disconnect personally and figure out why it does not sit comfortably with you. What line was crossed? Was it values-related, was it process-oriented? Do so with clarity. One additional point: under no circumstance should you hesitate to immediately raise clearly unacceptable behaviour (bullying, intimidation, harassment and so on) with relevant departments. Every company should have an established internal (and often external) complaint process. It should be used wherever and whenever needed.

- **Appreciate:** while it's often difficult when in the moment, get into the habit of appreciating the value of such an experience. Despite the initial heartache, it is a gift, so treat it like one.

- **Document:** make sure you document your experiences in a way that is easily accessible, crystal clear and confidential. I keep a private data folder labelled 'Bad Boss/Valued Experiences'. I have a one-page template for recording instances of note: I outline the situation at hand (who, when and what), alongside one to three insights to take away. It's an easy reference for future reminders.

- **Socialise:** spread what you've learned far and wide. We all know the power of storytelling, and practical first-hand examples are perfect for lifelong learning. You have a responsibility to share these invaluable learnings. Do so with openness, passion and conviction. Maintain respect (and legality) by removing the names of the individuals in question.

- **Consider:** constructive feedback to the boss in question, ideally in the moment. Warning — do so authentically and respectfully. If it's delivered poorly, you could be in for a world of pain! Some bad bosses simply have blind spots and are not aware of them. With constructive feedback, leaders can address these blind spots and improve.

MODEL FOR THE WHITEBOARD

Blind Spots

Created by psychologists Joseph Luft and Harrington Ingham way back in 1955, figure 8.2 is a great model to consider when giving feedback to a bad boss. It allows you to truly be inquisitive as to what blind spots are in existence in yourself and others. I find it an exceptional coaching and feedback model.

From your own perspective, ask yourself why you have these blind spots. Ideally, you want to discover these unknowns and eventually, through transparency, you can also deepen the quadrant marked 'open' and reduce the dreaded 'façade' quadrant.

Interestingly, I have seen some people divide the façade quadrant in two: one side remains 'façade' but the other is labelled 'secret'.

	Known to self	Not known to self
Known to others	**Open**	**Blind spot** *Upon uncovering a blind spot, remind yourself that self awareness is different from self development. If you believe it is worth addressing, then do somethinig about it. Most do not.*
Not known to others	**Façade** *Façades often relate to the dreaded Imposter Syndrome. They help no-one. Secrets, on the other hand, are just downright dangerous.*	**Unknown** *This is the quadrant of breakthrough, transformation and possibility. Search deep.*

Figure 8.2: blind spots: the Johari window

What I like about that approach is that, for the majority of us, we put on a façade to hide our own perceived limitations and weaknesses from others (yet again, the ever-present imposter syndrome). The 'secret' section, however, is much more sinister. It's about hiding something factual from others that could jeopardise trust, relationships or positions of power.

For reference, I also use the same model when doing strategic planning sessions. I replace 'self' with 'us' (i.e. the team or company), and 'others' with 'competitors' or 'industry'. It makes you search for deeper understanding that can lead to breakthrough.

Plus, it's very easy to draw up quickly on a whiteboard!

THE CRITIQUE

A brief review from Global Leadership Executive Adviser Jack Jefferies, Colorado, USA.

....

Bad bosses are just that, bad bosses.

And though they may keep life interesting, they rarely add much value. In fact, poor leadership erodes culture, disengages people and ultimately destroys value. It is true that the difficult lessons about 'how not to lead' embed themselves deeply in our minds. They are lessons that have often been learned the hard way, through emotionally painful experience that is never to be forgotten and always to be avoided. And therein lies the rub. Sometimes, under certain circumstances, what can be perceived as a negative leadership behaviour may be downright necessary, if it is demonstrated in a situationally appropriate manner.

In my experience, I have observed a surprisingly common pattern— where a leader is allergic to demonstrating a critical competency because they consider it wrong, sometimes immoral. When I ask why the aversion, I often hear a story about how a prior boss had abused said competency by either over-using it, applying it in a clumsy manner or having bad motivations. After experiencing the boss's poor behaviour, the executive had sworn an oath to never repeat it. When taken to extreme, the executive wilfully refuses to exercise much-needed leadership and consequently fails at their job.

Catherine suffered from this failing. She rose to a regional GM role through reliably delivering results. Her boss was a political animal. He spent most of his time 'smooching' global leadership, all the while neglecting his team. He would make demands, offer little support, and point fingers at his team when the region did not deliver. As a result, Catherine and her peers felt hung out to dry.

Years later, I was assigned to coach this talented GM after she was promoted to president of another region. After one year in the role Catherine was failing because she was unable to convince the global team on the merits of her strategy and unable to obtain the resources her region required. After reviewing feedback from the global team, I asked Catherine about the quality of her relationships with senior leaders beyond her region and how much time she spent interacting with them. Her response was remarkable in its naivety: 'Why would I spend time at global headquarters? My people need me here!'

Catherine had learned the lesson from her prior boss that 'politics are bad'. After witnessing bad political behaviour and personally experiencing the negative consequences, she swore never to be political herself. When she was promoted into a role that required political savvy, she studiously avoided the necessary relationship-building and networking needed to get her good ideas put to use.

Ingraining lessons from bad bosses in your memory and ensuring you never repeat them can be taken too far. 'Negativity bias' can create a visceral aversion, making you dogmatic about your beliefs. Seeing the world as black-and-white or all-or-nothing is a sure way to stall your career.

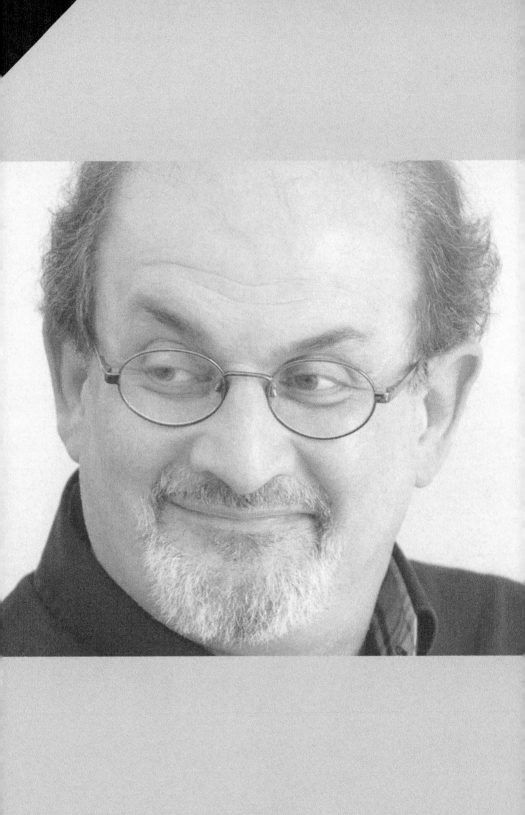

Chapter 9
The 3 A's (and one critical E)

I used to feel sorry for my remote-based teams.

The isolated markets, the field sales crew, the regional office folk, those poor souls working on night shift away from the masses.

Distanced from the buzz and hype of head office, from the hourly meetings, the water cooler conversations, the coaching and training and the constant influx of visitors and revolving presentations.

Poor buggers.

I changed my view of all that one day. Saw a chart from our engagement gurus: those furthest away from head office tended to have the highest engagement scores.

Interesting. I guess author Salman Rushdie was right when he said, 'Most of what matters in our lives takes place in our absence'.

THE MESSAGE ··························

If you get the opportunity to do a centralised role, do it. Be it a shared service function, a regional role or even global stardom, just say yes and get in there. How long you stay there is up to you. It may drive you absolutely crazy, and, very likely, you will make heaps of mistakes. But oh, the benefits: huge and far ranging. Perspective is instantly expanded, relationship builds are mandatory and negotiation and mediation are necessities.

Plus, your chance to see the world will be greatly amplified, always a cool thing when others are paying for it. When you do get back into a local role or operational market, you will be infinitely better. Conversely, if you have only ever done a global or centralised role, then please prepare to move and do so quickly. You need to become operational and appreciate local nuances. Until you experience a local role, you will never operate at your peak. And unless you do, both global and local will never win.

Those who are good in centralised roles have three common characteristics. I term these the 3 A's. You either do one of the three — ideally, all three — or you should do nothing at all. In the event you fail to perform any, then there is a fourth letter. Unfortunately, it doesn't start with an A and that is why I will never make money by being a smooth strategic consultant. This one starts with an E. It means stop doing everything and Exit before you do any more damage. Let's hope you never become an E.

And if you're currently in a local role? Well, this chapter equally relates. Unless your attitude and behaviours are perfectly aligned with others, suboptimal performance will be a given. You may get some occasional wins, yet seldom will they be enduring.

··

This chapter is a bit different: the 'practical steps' will be woven through-out, as will any strategic models of note. You need this chapter to work hard for you.

Why is this topic so important? Two reasons.

First, I cannot think of a topic that has involved more talk, frustration, angst and non-value distraction than this one. Distraction for myself, but equally to the people and teams around me. It does not matter if you are local, regional, global or central. Everyone is involved and everyone is affected.

Second, the benefits of effective collaboration between centralised and non-centralised teams are large. Significantly large. Although we seldom see it, a successful working model will deliver massive competitive advantages leading to healthier top and bottom lines. I'm convinced the model can work so much better than it does today. We see isolated examples of exceptional success and we need to replicate them. To do so, however, will require change.

Aside

It's interesting that as I'm writing this, I cannot help but think of the multiple projects that I have been involved in where we tried to achieve effective and efficient ways of working between centralised and non-centralised structures.

I have followed models, processes, procedures, systems, operational playbooks and organisational blueprints on so many occasions. They have come from some of the sharpest strategic minds in the world, leading consultants from Bain, BCG, McKinsey, IMD, Deloitte, and Accenture. They are very good at what they do, and they are, as they were once described to me, 'everything but cheap'.

Undeniably, there are exceptional benefits that come from following these recommendations. (If you do not derive benefit, it is likely that you have not implemented them with excellence.) Some will disagree.

When they see 'success shortfall', they lay blame on the consultants. I used to be like this, but now I think differently. In the vast majority of cases, leading strategic consultants—and I do say 'leading'—will invariably add and deliver the value they promise. If they don't, my first port of call is to look at myself in the mirror and ask what I did wrong and how I contributed to this position. And if by chance it is the actual fault of the consultants, I ask myself exactly the same questions. My mindset is very much if they fail, I fail.

With that said, let me now contradict myself.

Why is it, that even when we follow such exceptionally researched and proven success models, we end up feeling short-changed? Why is it that people from both sides of the equation still have daily frustrations, gripes and are constantly involved in non-value-adding distractions? Why do they blame each other when things go wrong and why is it a rarity for someone to put their hand up and say, 'It was me, I screwed up'?

My view should not surprise you: 'It's not always right to be right'.

Regardless of which best-practice template or academic playbook you follow, it will never matter unless you get the fundamental people principles working, and working early:

- relationships

- expectations

- mindsets

- alignment

- shared visions, purposes and agendas.

Unless you have these basics in play, regardless of having the perfect implementation program, you will fall short. These tips are not academic and are seldom included in a playbook. But by heck, I wish I had documented and used all of them a lot earlier.

CENTRALISATION STATION

Let us start with some clarity. What do I mean by 'centralisation'? Why is it beneficial and what are the current issues?

At some stage in your career, you will find yourself needing to manage or oversee a centralised type of role. There are numerous examples of what centralised roles look like. For the purpose of simplicity, let's think of them as being either global, regional or a shared function. Examples would include:

- responsibility for multiple markets

- accountability for a regional supply chain

- leadership of a global brand

- simply being part of the team servicing the IT, HR, logistics or financial requirements for a number of locally operated sites.

Either way, they are centralised in scope with the majority having a remit to service the needs of those around them.

I am a supporter of centralised functions. In most cases, the benefits of centralisation are crystal clear: through consistent alignment of strategy and objectives, we get everyone working towards the same goal. Increased cohesion means less duplication, and increased efficiency. Scale is always advantageous and, when working effectively, it is exceptionally hard to beat. When centralisation works, all stakeholders should be super positive. Big tick.

Here comes the sad part.

Despite doing numerous local, regional and global roles — within different geographies, companies and industry sectors — the aforementioned benefits result way less than one would like. I have learned over time that this is a common story.

So, what goes wrong and how can we make it right? And, while we're at it, what the hell are these 3 A's?

ASSIST, ADD VALUE OR ACCELERATE

I introduced this concept (see figure 9.1) some time ago.

Figure 9.1: the 3 A's (and one critical E)

It was with my Chicago-based Wrigley brand team and we were talking roles and responsibilities. The overarching premise was for the team to get into a customer-first mindset: how could they best service the needs of the 50-plus international markets that were relying on the global team for success? The message we agreed upon was that everything we did on a daily basis must fall within one of the 3 A's:

1. assist

2. add value

3. accelerate.

If we could not do any of these 3 A's, then we would have no choice other than to adhere to a simple E: we exit. We stop doing anything at all and, as a result, we stop doing potential harm.

Let me expand with the key questions that every centralised employee and team should ask themselves:

- 'Is what I'm doing **assisting** the local market (or team) in their quest for success?' If it's not, immediately stop doing it.

- 'Is the activity that I'm doing **adding value** to the market I'm servicing? Specifically, would the market say it's adding value?' If it's not, immediately stop doing it.

- 'Is what I'm doing **accelerating** the achievement of the plan for the market I'm servicing?' If it will not accelerate plan achievement, then stop doing it. Immediately.

I know that these questions seem basic. They are, but they're not always obvious. The resources that are wasted by centralised activity that does not assist, add value or accelerate plan achievement is massive. It makes a mockery of the quest for efficiency and distracts everyone from the bigger picture.

Let me be very clear that I do not think this is the sole fault or responsibility of the global or centralised team; far from it. When things aren't working, they are equally as frustrated as the local operational teams. This is definitely a collective issue that requires a collective solution.

In figure 9.2 (overleaf), I set out the main issues that I have experienced or witnessed within both local and centralised roles, along with commentary that addresses each of them.

You will notice at the base of this model, it portrays the desired mindset that effective collaboration entails, from a position of dependence to independence through to interdependence. Depending on the market maturity or desired strategic intent, companies will have different positions. This is perfectly allowable, so long as you are aware of where you currently lie and where you want to go.

OPERATIONAL/LOCAL TEAMS

I start with local teams because they're usually the ones who complain the most about their centralised counterparts. Sometimes it's justified, many times it is not. During my earlier years, I was a strong contributor to this commentary of complaint. It helps no-one. I believe there are four fundamental issues at play:

1. not seeing value
2. not invented here
3. not being transparent
4. not being appreciative.

Let's look closer at each of these.

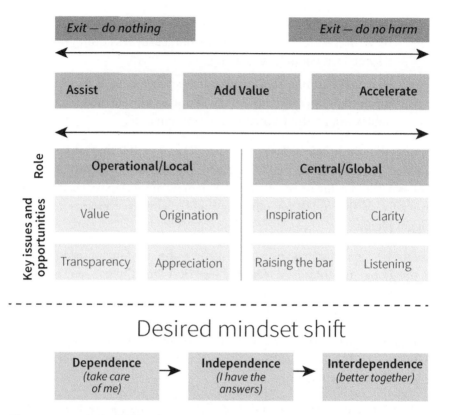

Figure 9.2: central–local operating principles

NOT SEEING VALUE

Many local teams have a mindset of independence. They believe they are in complete control of their destiny and have the resources, capabilities and know-how to succeed. They fundamentally believe they are better when they travel alone. The belief is amplified when that unit has had historical success. Worse still, in moments of crisis, many local units become more stoic and more individualistic than before — 'it's our responsibility and we will fix it'.

Unfortunately, this is flawed thinking.

Centralised teams often possess a wealth of experience, perspective and insight that can be invaluable to local operations. Additional resources should be actively sought, leveraged and welcomed with open arms. Especially in moments of crisis where fresh eyes are always needed.

Furthermore, local teams should realise the benefit of scale. When a centralised activity is executed well, costs are spread far and wide. It allows local markets and teams to focus on what they do well. Executing with excellence.

RECOMMENDED APPROACH

Request, demand and leverage central resources whenever possible. Good organisations will manage resource complexity with ease so never use this as an excuse. Finally, under no circumstances pull back in times of crisis.

A word of advice

I mention in chapter 3 that I want my teams to strive for an 'unfair share' of exceptional talent. I give them exactly the same request in regard to the number of resources that they should be securing from centralised teams. Local teams usually get cross-charged (specific dollar costs) for their use of central services, so always strive for an unfair share of their resource base.

NOT INVENTED HERE

This can best be described as follows: 'Regardless of how good a concept, initiative or strategy is, unless it was invented by us, it'll never be good enough.'

Despite the massive benefits of scale and efficiency coupled with the significant freeing up of local resources, great activities just get overlooked because they 'weren't invented here.' This is beyond frustrating. More infuriating is the amount of wasted time and resources taken by local teams in justifying why the global initiative won't work and the local one will. It is a waste of resources that offers no benefit to a customer, supplier or consumer.

Aside

My own guilt for this topic relates back to my marketing days in Reebok Europe. The head of Global Marketing at the time was very good at what she did, but I always thought I was better. If she went right, I would go left. If she said fashion, I would say performance. If she went mainstream broadcast, I would go digital. You get the point.

I got away with this for two reasons. I had a boss who shielded and protected me from the inevitable protests and I also had good growth and results within Europe. I was very lucky on both fronts. My focus should have been on true partnership and support to the global team. I should have been a provider of inspiration, thought leadership and working efficiencies. Brenda, my apologies. I definitely learned from these experiences and changed my behaviours accordingly.

RECOMMENDED APPROACH

When a central initiative comes your way, ensure that you and your teams start with a default position of 'why not' as opposed to 'why'. On occasions, the activity will not be suitable, yet ensure these are the exceptions and definitely not the rule.

Furthermore, ensure that you and your teams understand the true costs of 'going it alone'. Ask the question, 'Are the finite resources of my local team better served on development and origination of an initiative, or better deployed towards executional excellence?' Do a 'time in motion' study on what it takes to develop a new strategic initiative from scratch. You will be amazed at the considerable time and resources involved.

NOT BEING TRANSPARENT

If you've done a stint in sales, you will know the concept of a 'dog and pony show'. It generally happens when you get a visit from the big boss or global team. You take them on a well-orchestrated market visit, during which your products and services are perfectly displayed for all to see. 'Nothing to see here, this is just the way it is 365 days of the year.'

In my case, it has looked like this:

- Every time a client visited the agency, their TV ad just happened to be blasting out in reception on an unusually large video screen with philharmonic-quality speakers.

- Every Reebok shoe and Greg Norman golf shirt would be elegantly displayed in the prime window position of the very leading sports and fashion outlet of the country being visited.

- The petrol station that we just so happened to pop into on our route from the airport to the office would feature a Wrigley merchandising stand positioned perfectly to the left of the cash register, lit to perfection with eye-pleasing down-lights and conveniently surrounded by three mouth-watering location displays of Eclipse Mints, Skittles and Starburst confections.

- And you know what, it just so happened that on that very day, next to that very store we just happened to be randomly visiting, there was a massive outdoor poster featuring one of our brands. Oh, and I almost forgot. That one store manager who just happened to be walking by was so overwhelmingly positive about the local team, the brands and the business in totality.

Uncanny.

We've all done it and I've been on both sides of the equation. Amusingly, not one central or global visitor doesn't know it either! It's one of the reasons that whenever the owners of the company used to visit us, it was pointless even attempting to cover all bases. You would stop where they wanted to stop, and seldom was it in the direction you were planning.

My message: There is absolutely no benefit in trying to hide the way things actually are from the central team. The comedic examples I listed are as relevant throughout the entire business as they are within sales.

Local businesses and GMs do everything in their power to ensure a central visit passes with no tension. They breathe a massive sigh of relief, 'high-five' the leadership team and tell their partners that evening over a glass of red wine, 'Well, thank God we survived that one.' This approach doesn't add value.

The real benefit of these visits is having people see your business for what it is. Central teams bring a fresh set of eyes and can provide invaluable perspective, but they can only do this if you are totally transparent and prepared to show your vulnerabilities — warts and all. I prefer red scorecards to green scorecards from these visits. It's exactly the same within a safety, quality or financial audit. Red scorecards identify problems that need to be addressed. They highlight something that you and your teams had not noticed before and demand attention. Red is a colour never to be fearful of.

RECOMMENDED APPROACH

Be transparent and vulnerable. It really is as simple as that. Encourage your teams to do the same. This does not mean you avoid pre-aligned objectives and messages that you want to get across to central visitors; these are critical. However, under no circumstances get into hide mode. During warehouse, factory and office floor walks, get employees to give open and honest assessments on how they think things are going. Have them openly share their views on safety, quality and efficiency. Have customers and partners tell it as it is. Real-time feedback, real insight, for real benefit.

There is a caveat. You need to make a contract with the central team prior to the visit.

My standard approach goes like this:

> The team is really looking forward to your visit. Everyone will be 100 per cent open and transparent. You will hear what is working and what is not. Where we do not have the answers, we will tell you. As a result, we will be vulnerable. I expect you to hold us to account; however, please do not be judgemental or overly critical as we will need partnership and support above anything else.

Finally, if the reasons stated are not enough to convince you to move away from the 'milk run' approach, ask yourself: 'How much focus am I removing from my business as a result of this distraction?' Enough said.

NOT BEING APPRECIATIVE

Having done a number of years within regional and global teams, I think this issue is bigger than we realise. When you're in a local gig, you're close to the action. When results come your way, you get a real buzz and a real sense of personal achievement. When you're in a centralised role, success is often a long way away. In many cases, you hear of results days, if not weeks, past their fruition. Accomplishments are not attributed to you or your teams — in some cases, you don't ever get a mention or an acknowledgement of your contribution.

You may be thinking, 'That's just the way it is and those central folk just gotta toughen up.' For those who do not need recognition from others, that's cool. But for the majority, acknowledgement of effort does matter.

RECOMMENDED APPROACH

Acknowledge, appreciate and recognise. Small things make a difference. Distance should never be a barrier to recognition, so please remind yourself and your teams of its importance.

Aside

You may be surprised at how little recognition or acknowledgement senior leaders receive from others. Great work or great deeds are often seen as expected and just part of a normal course of duty. True, senior leaders are paid exceptionally well and you hope that the quality of their decision making matches their salary. But the fact is, it can be lonely as a leader. Small recognition from all levels makes a massive difference to their energy levels. Of all the recognitions that I have received over the years, one of the more special ones happened about a year ago. A factory associate placed a handwritten note in my hands with the words, 'Kiwis can indeed fly'. I have kept that note and even 12 months on, I think of it often. Thank you, Jim. You are an exceptional man.

CENTRALISED/REGIONAL/GLOBAL TEAMS

Okay, this part is for all those in centralised roles. First and foremost, please do not forget the 3 A's. They are easy to do, surprisingly effective and absolutely critical. In addition, note the following four themes that require awareness and subsequent attention:

1. not being inspirational

2. not providing clarity

3. not raising the bar

4. not listening.

NOT BEING INSPIRATIONAL

The CEO of a respected UK telecommunications business told me the number one role of his leadership team was to inspire. To give unprecedented levels of energy to everyone they interacted with.

Every person who presented or interacted with his leadership team had to leave the meeting more energised than when they first entered. Most people who enter a senior meeting as a guest or a presenter will have a degree of apprehension: how will I perform, will there be tension, and will they derive insight? Imagine every individual walking out feeling more energised and more inspired than when they walked in. Sensational.

Upon being told this, I endeavour to do it on every occasion of interaction. Even during times when I have a critical but necessary message to deliver. I do not always succeed, but I always attempt to do so.

RECOMMENDED APPROACH

Use your centralised platform to inspire others. Make it a personal quest. The best way to do so is via purpose and vision. Local teams get immersed within operational detail. Remind and inspire them about the 'why' and make sure you do it in a compelling and creative way. Don't roll out standard corporate-speak — rather, think and act like a world-class marketeer.

My previous boss used to tell me that 'every interaction is an opportunity for impact'. Because of my outstanding listening skills, she needed to repeat this to me three times! It is a definite truism and one for all central teams to note.

Aside

In chapter 3, The man who used to smile, I mention Jack Jefferies, my favourite business coach (he also provided the critique on chapter 8). He, along with many others, talks of a concept called appreciative enquiry. I love the simplicity of the concept. Officially, it's a change management approach that focuses on:

- identifying what's working well

- analysing why it's working well

- then doing more of it.

The basic idea is that an organisation will grow in whichever direction its people focus their attention.

Jack talked about how he and his fellow US skydiving team leveraged this approach. After every 'safely landed' jump, they would gather together and debrief immediately. They started with appreciate enquiry, examining what worked individually and what worked collectively as a team. They then made an agreement to do these things again. But for the next jump, they would do them even better.

Many sports teams use appreciative enquiry with great effect. One of the easiest ways of doing this is pulling together a highlights package from various games throughout the season. It showcases those moments and examples of individual and team brilliance: strength in mid-week training and preparation; game time decision making; calmness and composure in periods of difficulty; selfless acts promoting team unity; and often strength and humility upon a successful end result. I know it's a cliché, yet sports and business philosophies are so intertwined. Practices of this nature are equally applicable to your teams and your organisations. Consider this approach as a way of inspiring local teams on what they are doing with brilliance.

NOT PROVIDING CLARITY

Clarity of purpose, vision, mission and strategic direction is critical for any business. For local teams, it is essential. Even if your strategic choices are not perfect — and let's face it, they never will be — as long as they are clearly articulated, easy to understand and compelling, you have a strong likelihood of success.

When a central team provides clarity to local units, they know:

- why they are here

- what targets they are striving for

- what choices have been made.

They also know the key enablers and behaviours required to succeed. There is little debate or distraction, with attention focused on what they do and how they best do it.

A word of advice

I have been most effective within regional and global roles when I focus on strategic alignment ahead of executional detail. If I can get a local unit fully aligned with strategic direction, the rest is easy. Central teams often focus on gaining alignment on activities. As we have discussed, gaining global scale with activities is important, yet it should always be secondary after cohesion of strategy.

Once a local unit is fully on board with strategy, they will generally get behind global activities. Especially when you show the success being achieved by other units or markets that are using them.

Another area relating to clarity is that of expectations. Specifically around roles, responsibilities and decision making. Without up-front clarification of who does what, it's almost impossible to deploy talent with optimal efficiency. Within most of my interactions at different CEO forums, both local and global teams within multinationals state it as one of their most pressing issues.

RECOMMENDED APPROACH

Provide a simple, compelling and relevant strategic plan to local markets. This has to be a priority ahead of any executional discussions. Everyone has their own model preferences; mine is featured on my website www.hamishrthomson.com. Once provided, focus on ensuring complete unit alignment.

Set expectations early for both central and local teams. Determine what is important to each party, how best that need is served and agree who should deliver what and by when.

Document what has been agreed upon, socialise it with all relevant personnel and collectively make it happen. Agree on set review dates and, where needed, update and revise accordingly. This should also include alignment on what decision-making process is to be followed and who has the final decision rights on set topics. This is simple stuff that makes a big difference and saves a lot of heartache.

One other area: I am a firm believer in a 'shared agenda'. Do not expect people to automatically connect with one another unless there is a valid reason to do so. This is relevant for individuals but also teams, departments and indeed markets and regions. Give them a shared purpose and a shared topic to collectively address and collaboration will be a given. It can also be an outstanding unlocker of hidden talent within lower layers of an organisation. People can delight and surprise on a wider stage and, for some, it can be the making of their career.

NOT RAISING THE BAR

One of the first tasks that a central team will do is try to bring all local units up to an acceptable level of performance. This may be total unit performance on growth, profit or cash. Equally it could pertain to specific performance relating to customer service levels, days of supply, safety metrics or market penetration levels. High-performing organisations will set a benchmark at the level of the highest performing unit, deploying central resources to assist those markets below the desired line. I support this approach, yet I have one critical concern: it's like playing catch-up football. It doesn't lift the bar to new heights of acceptable performance levels.

Let me clarify with the help of this hypothetical model (see figure 9.3):

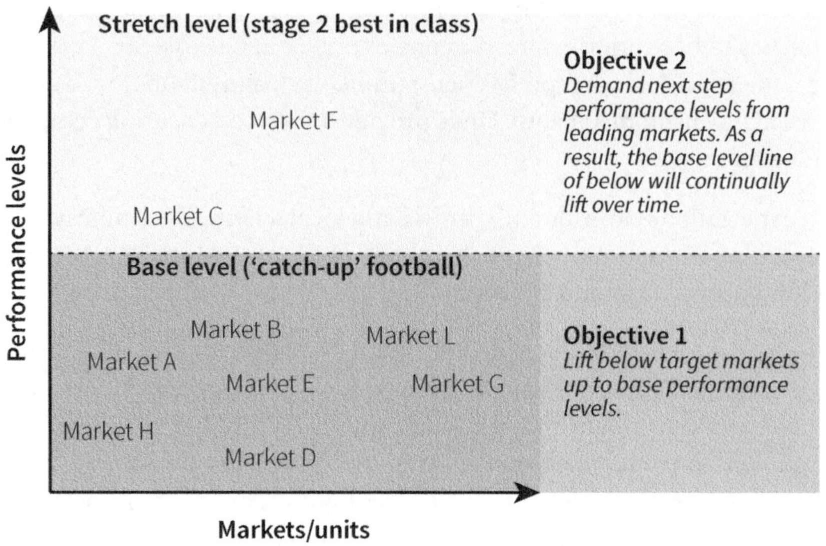

Stretch level (stage 2 best in class)

Performance levels

Market F

Market C

Objective 2
*Demand next step
performance levels from
leading markets. As a
result, the base level line
of below will continually
lift over time.*

- - - - - **Base level ('catch-up' football)** - - - - -

Market B

Market A

Market E

Market H

Market D

Market L

Market G

Objective 1
*Lift below target markets
up to base performance
levels.*

Markets/units

Figure 9.3: raising the bar on market/unit expectations

As you can see, the majority of the markets are below the 'base level' horizontal line. By the time they lift themselves up to that base line, competitors will have forged ahead and created a new level of desired performance (i.e., they will already be at the 'stretch level' line in figure 9.3). They will have discovered new ways of working that make the original base line redundant. In effect, this means that the rest of us are simply raising levels to the lowest common denominator.

This alone is not a major insight. Effective global leaders and teams are aware of this already and, naturally, they want continuous improvements in performance. They will demand that their high-performing markets (for example, markets like 'C' and 'F' in figure 9.3) strive for next-level performance. They will inspire lead markets to push boundaries, be curious and establish new best practice for everyone else to follow.

It's the correct request to make, yet it is meaningless unless resources are allocated to make it reality. Without necessary resources, success will be lucky at best.

The resources need to be either carved out of the central team or reallocated by the local team. Reallocation will usually mean something else is temporarily sacrificed, and this needs to be agreed and contracted between parties.

For some, I appreciate that this may feel like a 'nice to do' and simply getting into unnecessary and boring detail. My focus, however, as a central or local leader, will always be about raising benchmarks. Averaging is important but it will never promote extraordinary.

Finally, a last point on raising the bar: use your markets in exactly the same way you use your brand portfolio. They play different roles with different methodologies for success. Identify what markets will be your challenger brands — new ways of working, new models and new 'go to market' strategies. Multiple markets allow true risk and experimentation so benefit accordingly.

RECOMMENDED APPROACH

Continue setting the bar for all local units on an acceptable level of performance. Do not deviate from this — the internal competition among peers alone is invaluable. Provide central resources and support to achieve this and ensure adequate local deployment. At the same time, identify specific local units to raise the bar to the next level. Demand and inspire them to do this. Ideally, you carve out set global resources to make this happen. If these resources are not available, provide the market in question 'relief' by allowing resources to be reallocated. Do the same for all areas of globalisation, with an ongoing mindset of always raising the bar.

NOT LISTENING

Active listening has never been a strength of mine. I listen with what I believe is outstanding intent, yet way too often I'm already in solution mode as I'm doing so. This has made me less effective than I could have been.

RECOMMENDED APPROACH

There is no silver bullet to this area, with only one request for all central folk. Seek to understand before being understood. It matters more than ever when entering local situations that are removed from your everyday.

I have only skimmed the surface of this topic. I have learned considerably from others over the years on what to do and also what not to do. For those with whom I have worked on both sides of the equation, thank you for your patience and, importantly, thank you for the learnings.

THE CRITIQUE

A brief review from April Palmerlee, former US diplomat and current CEO of the American Chamber of Commerce, Australia.

Being right is overrated.

Everyone wants to be right, even when it comes at the expense of cultural sovereignty, corporate productivity, group cohesion or another's feelings. Intrinsic in our need to be right is the desire to put ourselves above others. In this case, to think that global HQ knows better than those in the regions. Or vice versa.

However, there are several things that should be at least as important, and probably more important, than being right. It takes most people a long time to learn this lesson. Once the fact is recognised, though, decisions come faster and easier, and relationships are more productive and harmonious. And usually, no harm (other than to one's ego) is done by forgoing the need to be right.

Those 'other things' include being receptive and accepting of difference. Cultural experience and my diplomatic roles have taught me this. Regardless of origin, diversity of views is essential. It also includes curiosity. What do others have, and what can they offer? Without curiosity, regions, countries and companies would never explore and seldom partner.

The responsibility to say 'yes' — to make decisions that will benefit other team members or customers — does not lie solely with the boss at global headquarters. Everyone in the organisation, including in remote offices, should be empowered to do the right thing, without waiting for permission or direction. Openness, kindness, objectivity and humility should go both ways.

Of course, the benefits of strong direction from the centre are clear: a consistent alignment of strategies and objectives will lead everyone to work efficiently and effectively towards the same goal. Efficiency at scale is hard to beat.

And that is what makes this chapter so important: recognising that it is incumbent on all of us, whether we have already achieved a lofty position in the corporate hierarchy or are recent graduates just starting out, whether we sit in New York or New Zealand, whether we are part of the chairman's office or the smallest outpost, to take actions that assist, add value or accelerate progress.

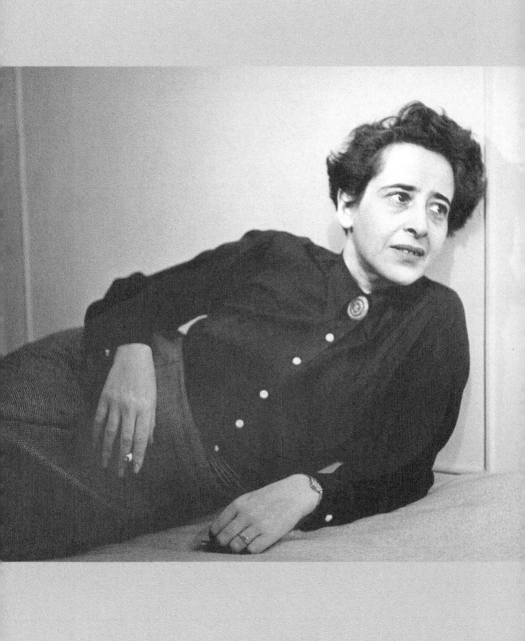

Chapter 10

It Only Hurts When You Write the Cheque

Hannah Arendt is widely considered one of the most important political philosophers of the twentieth century.

She was an important interpreter of her time: someone who fostered continuous reading and rereading of her work. And someone whose ideas and concepts still help those dealing with current realities.

I like to apply her quote, 'There are no dangerous thoughts: thinking itself is dangerous,' to over-thinking and over-intellectualising.

Sometimes, it pays to have a go and just get on with it.

THE MESSAGE ··························

To be totally transparent, this concept probably shouldn't make the chapter list. Unless I ramble, it should take me a couple of short paragraphs to explain. There's no theory, no model and no expert critiques: just a cool term I reference when I find myself in a state of indecision.

Probably around six years ago, I was going through the process of buying a car. I like cars. Ideally fast ones, but there's always the trade-off regarding cash. Should I be sensible and honourable and buy an affordable four-door family sedan, be the perfect partner and help pay down the mortgage? For some unknown reason, it seldom works like this for me. Maddie says she knows the reason, but that's for another story. When wrestling with the 'yea or nay' decision (to buy or not to buy), I was on the phone with one of my brothers back in New Zealand — the middle one. He also likes cars. His point was simple: 'Mate, it only hurts when you write the cheque'.

Hard to argue: the pain is generally temporary.

··

So how does this relate to business?

Well, how many times have you had drawn-out discussions about those 'over and above' dollars needed to retain or attract the very best talent to your organisation? When they work out, and most do, I don't think I have ever said, 'Shame we paid that little bit more'. Nope, I don't remember ever saying it or even thinking it. Same relates to the money spent on production budgets, capital equipment, acquisitions, conferences and office refurbs. Consistent with family holidays, birthday presents, weekend breaks and music festivals: there is never a perfect time for these things, and some of them end up costing you a small fortune. But at the end of the day, once you have written that abhorrently painful cheque, most of the time we only remember the up side from there on in.

Thanks Nige — sage advice with absolutely no substance to back it up. Exactly why I like it.

P.S. I got the fast car.

Chapter 11
Get a Life

You have to be incredibly brave, methodical and disciplined to strive for and achieve balance. Philippe Petit, French high-wire artist extraordinaire, said, 'My journey has always been the balance between chaos and order'.

Most of us can only sit back, admire and wonder.

We talk, we preach, we debate, we oscillate.

We do, we don't, we master, we stumble.

Live to work or work to live?

A deceptively simple question.

THE MESSAGE ·························

Some people live to work and others work to live. It doesn't matter which side of the ledger you're on; what matters is that you're aware of the consequences, both good and bad, of choosing either path. The consequences for not only yourself, but the messaging you send to other aspiring leaders.

I want this chapter to do two things. First, I want it to provide you confidence that leadership does not always mean sacrifice. This will be difficult to achieve, yet I am convinced it is true. Second, I want it to issue a reminder that every leader is responsible for role-modelling effective life–work balance. Challenging as this is, I know with certainty that it can be done. I also know with conviction that it *must* be done.

···

Where to start?

Maybe we commence with detailing the many reasons why people believe leadership means sacrifice. The greater the success, the greater the impact. The higher the position, the higher the burden. You get the picture. When we rise up the corporate ladder, we're under more pressure and invariably, home life can get smashed.

Yes, I could start there but I will not. That is too easy, too obvious and collectively, we have seen more than enough examples to add validity. I want to talk about and showcase the opposite: those leaders who make balance work, and *how* they make it work.

I have been inspired and led by many of these very leaders who make balance work. Leaders of different cultures, genders and personal circumstances, who have had unbelievable breadth and scope of responsibility, accountability levels that most people would shudder at, workloads that defy belief and an intensity of pressure that is constant and unequivocally relentless.

Yet, they achieve and, importantly, portray balance. They passionately believe that *to create excellence at work, they must ultimately create excellence in life*. They realise that if they get this balance wrong, they will never deliver on their full potential, and exceptional leaders despise unfulfilled potential.

Aside

Austrian social psychologist Fritz Heider is credited with the idea of 'balance theory'. His 1950s notion is that we want to maintain psychological stability, and, as a result, we form relationships that balance our likes and dislikes. Essentially, balance means life is good; imbalance means a position of discomfort. Knowing this is easy. Getting optimal balance and showcasing that balance to others is the hard part.

So, how do these inspirational leaders do it?

With discipline. They provide the same diligence, focus and dedication to life–work balance as they do to the bottom line, if not more. Effective leaders:

- **ensure uninterrupted quality family time.** It is not up for debate. This time is scheduled, set aside and viewed as sacred. This includes taking regular and set holidays.

- **socialise.** With work colleagues or those outside the business; either way, it is regular, it is downtime and it is enjoyable.

- **exercise.** This does not necessarily mean flogging yourself to exhaustion, yet they believe in physical strength being a conduit to cognitive performance.

- **watch what they eat.** Some are extreme, most are balanced. On occasions, some even eat kale.

- **have perspective.** They are curious outside of what they know. They appreciate that interests and variety outside of work have subconscious benefits. They always do.

- **have connection.** Be that with community, country or the world at large.

- **value recovery.** They appreciate they are corporate athletes and that recovery is the cornerstone of enduring success. How they recover depends on the individual: for some it's meditation, for others it's music or reading. For many, it's wine.

- **have purpose and are purposeful.** Productivity and performance are one thing; doing good for a greater cause is another.

This is of course an incomplete list. There is a multitude of impressive and inspirational techniques and options available. Additionally, virtually every effective leader I have encountered has also had an exceptional support base around them. Be that at home or at work, they often need this to ensure they are at their peak. Without this support, it is challenging at best.

Personally, through trial and error, I now believe I am closer to achieving effective balance. When I commit to actions such as those listed, I am a better leader of myself and of others. My energy levels are high, I seldom have dreaded 'off days' and my enthusiasm and drive are palpable throughout an organisation. As a result, outside of work, I am a better partner, father and friend. Do I get it wrong at times? Hell, yes. But through awareness, education and experience, I am so much better than I used to be.

Everyone will have their own list and their own levels of importance in what constitutes effective balance. It will always depend on personal circumstance. For some, this will mean family first. For others it may be financial security or health. Understandably, most lists will also change over time.

Aside

Erik Erikson was a famous German-American developmental psychologist and psychoanalyst. He coined the phrase 'identity crisis' and maintained that personality develops in a predetermined order from infancy to adulthood. During each stage, the person experiences a crisis that could have a positive or negative outcome for personality development.

Recently I have been taking this concept more seriously. In particular, stage 7, generativity versus stagnation. It takes place during middle adulthood, from the ages of 40 to 65; in essence, generativity means you 'make your mark' on the world by creating or nurturing things that will outlast you. It means giving back and being part of a bigger picture. Success leads to feelings of usefulness and accomplishment, while failure (stagnation) can result in a feeling of inadequate involvement in the wider world. Above all, it's about finding purpose. This to me is exactly what life–work balance is about. The frustration is that most of us have to reach our forties or fifties to discover it.

TIME ON THE BALL

At the risk of oversimplification, have you ever noticed that some people are able to handle pressure so much better than others? On many occasions, they face exactly the same pressures as their peers, yet their response is noticeably different. No stress, and little anxiety or inertia in making key decisions. In sports, they term this as having 'time on the ball'. Despite everything coming at them, exceptional athletes never appear to be rushed; they absorb pressure with apparent ease. Dan Marino, Liz Ellis, Lionel Messi, Sam Kerr, Lewis Hamilton, Dan Carter. The list is long and impressive.

It's exactly the same in corporate life. Outstanding leaders have a knack of taking in pressure and remaining calm. Where needed, they shield pressure from others and remain super balanced. It's little wonder that these are the types of leaders that people aspire to be.

Interestingly, in high-pressure situations, the most composed person in the room is routinely the leader. This happens for a reason: time in role and experience are invaluable, and very few who translate pressure into stress reach the upper echelons of the corporate ladder.

You may have noticed that I consistently use the term 'life-work' balance, not the other way around.

I was drawn to this terminology via the former global CEO of Unilever, Paul Polman. He has spoken strongly of life-work balance and it resonated with me immediately.

Personally, I work to live; work is a means and not an end. Don't get me wrong—work is a very important part of who I am. It drives me, energises me and, critically, it inspires me. But it is only one part of me, and unless the rest falls into place, I will never be at my best for myself or as a leader of others.

THE IMPORTANCE OF MESSAGING

This brings me to my second desire for the chapter: a reminder of leadership responsibility.

Leaders of all levels have a responsibility to showcase an effective life–work balance. Unless they do so, those beneath them won't aspire to leadership. If you don't believe me, consider the following story.

One lasting memory comes from a town hall meeting I attended in Guangzhou, China many years ago. (A town hall meeting is what Americans call a briefing of sorts to employees or constituents, with opportunities for feedback and questions.)

Approximately 700 employees were in attendance. The session was being led by a company veteran of almost 40 years, an exceptional leader who at the time was the global lead of a multibillion-dollar segment. Much admired and uniformly respected, he was what I would call a 'super classy' leader. You knew exactly where he stood on all matters; he was a genuinely good bloke, and one of the most supportive, pragmatic and disciplined thinkers I have encountered.

On this one occasion, though, I did not agree with his messaging.

Following a general business update, questions were being taken from the floor. The first came from a mid-level sales manager from the southern province of Guangdong. He asked, 'Please can you tell me how you maintain a good level of work–life balance?'

It's a fairly standard question, and I was curious as to the response. The entire Chinese team had a reputation for being incredibly hardworking. They did long hours, with an accepted norm that you stayed in the office until your boss left. Many of the senior executives at the time had families based in other major cities or Asian countries, so during the working week they would regularly stay late in the office and get in early in the morning. No complaints were made; it was simply the way it was.

The response at the time was casual, humourous and honest: 'My wife will tell you there is no such thing as work–life balance, and, if there ever was such a thing, I certainly don't have it.'

He then proceeded to talk about the many promotions and assignments that had come his way. It was an impressive and inspirational list. Nobody had ever forced him to take these positions; he knew what he was getting into and believed the increased workload was simply part and parcel of more senior roles.

I understand this. It's a common practice within most large multinationals and is inherently true for most businesses, regardless of size and scale. That said, this response concerned me. I felt it delivered the wrong message to all the aspiring leaders in the room that day — including myself.

In the moment, I turned to my Corporate Affairs Director. Without needing to say anything, we just looked at each other and raised our eyebrows. It was clear she was thinking exactly the same as I was: 'Why the heck would you want to get to the top of the corporate ladder if that's the kind of sacrifice you have to make?'

At the time of that town hall, I was doing okay career-wise. I was heading up the Wrigley Pacific operation and we were approaching our fifth year of consecutive profitable growth — not bad for a so-called 'mature' region. I was a senior member of a dynamic Asia Pacific Leadership team that knew no boundaries. I had direct control over a couple of factories, multiple industry-leading gum, mint and confectionery brands, and was surrounded by an exceptionally passionate and talented team. But I'll tell you this, for those few minutes of that town hall meeting, there was not a chance I wanted to go further up the career ladder. If that was what it was going to take to get to the very top, count me out.

Over the years I have hypothetically discussed the China example with senior leaders and business coaches to mixed results.

The majority believe that authenticity is always the best approach, and that this leader was simply being honest and transparent. As I hope this book is demonstrating, authenticity is a key value of mine; yet in examples like this one, I feel a slightly revised tack is required.

I believe that the role of all leaders is to unlock potential in others. This includes encouraging career progression. Unless your leadership positively displays balance, many under your tutelage will never yearn for increased levels of seniority. If this means shielding some of your actual behaviours from others, so be it. I know this sounds disingenuous, yet I believe it's necessary.

Aside

An interview way back in 2002 with Australian swimming legend Ian Thorpe reminds me of the power that individuals have (or have not) in inspiring others around them to be their very best. Thorpe had just split from his long-time coach, Doug Frost. Together, they had amassed 17 individual world records and three Olympic gold medals: an impressive relationship by any standards. More astounding than the split itself was that Thorpe was replacing Frost with Frost's former assistant and high school arts teacher Tracey Menzies. The swimming fraternity and national press went into meltdown: who was this relatively inexperienced and unknown person to lead one of our greatest ever sporting icons?

Ignoring whether the change in coaches was successful or not (you be the judge—a bronze, silver and two gold medals at the 2004 Athens games, seven national titles, numerous World Championship and Grand Prix wins, coupled with Thorpe being the first man in history to win a medal in the 100 metre, 200 metre and 400 metre freestyle events at a single Olympic games), the part of the story that stood out to me was this. When Thorpe was asked the recurring question of why he chose her, he responded with, 'I see more potential in Tracey than she sees in herself'.

Wow. This is exceptional and inspirational leadership. The confidence boost she would have received from this one comment would have been massive. Would his response have placed additional pressure on her? Yes, I believe so, but let's face it, the pressure levels were off the charts from the very second that he announced he was making a change. His response would have lifted her game significantly.

One simple comment and I suspect a key reason for her continued success, which included being awarded New South Wales, Australia, Woman of the Year in 2005.

A QUESTION OF CHOICE

Prior to diving into the practical part, for those 'balance' sceptics out there, let me reiterate one thing.

I am not against those who prioritise work first. It's an individual choice. Recently, I worked out that I have travelled on average two days a working week since the age of 23. My latter years in Australia have been a lot more forgiving, which played a key role in my decision to return to this side of the world. My earlier years in Europe were particularly demanding: almost three-quarters of my time was spent on travel, with regular two- to three-week international trips. Without a home support base, this would have been impossible. I once did the numbers: I have missed out on 1536 days of the life of my youngest child, Evie. At age 16, that is 26 per cent of her life. Devastating.

Compared to those who serve in the forces, do uncompromising shift work or have work assignments many miles from home, I know my numbers pale in significance. Nevertheless, it still hurts. Even though I am super close to my kids, the guilt pangs still remain.

Aside

Encouragingly, some leaders reject the notion that there needs to be a trade-off between life and work in the first place. I find myself falling into this camp. Jappreet Sethi, who is the CEO of HexGn, referenced this in a 2014 article that I still have a printed copy of today. He suggested that even using the term 'work–life balance' implies there is a trade-off.

Additionally, if authentic leadership is about being the same person at work as you are at home, then surely one can complement the other. Psychologists call this the spillover effect, where desirable qualities transfer from one side to the other.

THE PRACTICAL PART

Life–work Balance

So many models, so many techniques. This framework (see figure 11.1) simply provides a starting point.

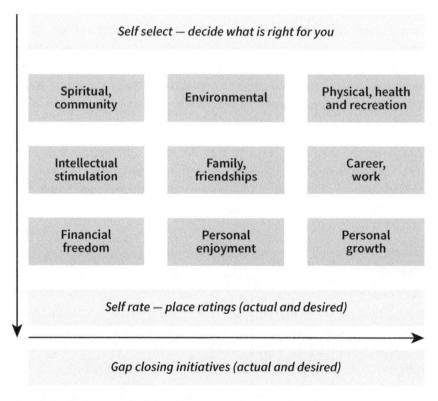

Figure 11.1: life-work dimensions — many and varied

To help find the right balance, take these steps:

- **Start with self-selection.** From the list in figure 11.1, determine which dimensions of balance are important to you. This is not an exhaustive list, so feel free to add anything that you feel is missing. Importantly, decide what's right for you at this particular point in time.

- **Self-rate the importance of each dimension.** A simple 1–10 scale will do. If family, career or health are critical to you, place as a 10. If finances, community and environment mean little at present, place as a 2.

- **Follow this up with an honest assessment** of where you sit today in terms of fulfilling these values. If you're feeling bold, do this with your partner, family or friends. I review my life–work progress once a year with Maddie. It can be a brutal but necessary reality check.

- **Develop a specific action plan to close identifiable gaps.** Commit and review as you see fit.

A few additional considerations:

- **Identify early warning signs of imbalance.** You want these to be leading indicators: observable areas that you, and others, can use to identify early signs of imbalance. I call these early alarm bells. In my case, this means being noticeably irritable. A lack of patience, an out-of-character snap or outburst, jumping into solution mode, cutting down discussions before reaching dialogue and just being a grumpy old bugger. Irritability: not my best trait.

- **Get back on track.** Everyone will have their own ways to do this. I use the mindfulness technique of going to my 'third space'. For some people, this means doing meditation, listening to music, going for a walk, having a coffee with friends or simply reading a good book. Whatever your chosen path, it is an immediate distraction from the issue at hand

and allows you to refocus and reenergise within an environment that works for you. It also puts pressure situations and tension points in perspective.

My 'third space' is physical exercise. I am not a gym junkie, yet following a run, swim, or game of tennis, I immediately feel revitalised. Things that had been preoccupying me immediately drop down the importance ladder and when I do refocus on them, I tend to address them with increased clarity and conviction.

- If everything else fails, **always remember to swallow the chill pill**. As Maddie has told me over many a year, 'chill out, it's only dog food'. (Before pet lovers get up in arms, she has also said the same to me about advertising, sports shoes, chewing gum, confections, rice and tomato sauce. Although I haven't told her so, she is correct on this.)

- **Identify your role model behaviours.** If you are leading others, this is about identifying those daily actions that will be noticed and perceived by others. The overarching principle is that small things matter. As a leader, they always do.

MODELS FOR THE WHITEBOARD

Energy Management

I mention the importance of energy in chapter 2, Drains and radiators. Undeniably, effective management of energy levels will enable a strong life-work balance. There are many methodologies available to help get you to the top of your game and stay there. One that I frequently leverage is that of figure 11.2. It is a common model that encompasses four leading components of energy—physical, emotional, mental and spiritual. Each component will play a different role throughout both your career and your life journey, and you will likely tap into each level at one point or another. I encourage you to explore the many energy management systems that are on offer (just take a look online) as they can be very beneficial, practical and relevant to follow.

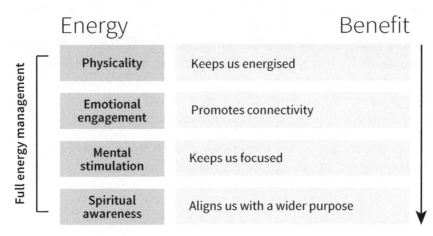

Figure 11.2: energy management
Adapted from The Power of Full Engagement *by Jim Loehr and Tony Schwartz, The Human Performance Institute.*

Aside

A few years back, a Canadian friend and former colleague of mine took a break from the corporate world and dedicated two years of his life preparing for Ironman.

I recall Bruce saying, 'Just like the corporate world, the two biggest insights are that you must have a good coach and recovery is more important than training'.

His second insight surprises people. In sports, intensity often comes in short bursts with good allowable recovery in between. In business, apart from the annual holiday, down time is often a luxury. Thus, your speed of recovery is absolutely essential.

I once had the good fortune of being a passenger in a two-seater Formula 1 Minardi car. Being driven around Melbourne's Albert Park circuit at breakneck speed was an experience I will never forget. The lesson drummed into me that day was that exceptional drivers are those with the ability to immediately recover from mistakes. The average driver will take multiple corners to get back on the perfect racing line following an indiscretion; the outstanding driver is back to perfection immediately. When you are talking in terms of a tenth-of-a-second difference between outstanding and average, you know the importance of recovery.

Even for us boring corporate bodies, being aware of this recovery process and adapting accordingly can get us significant benefits.

THE CRITIQUE

A brief rebuttal from leadership expert, author and women's advocate Fabian Dattner, Founder of the Dattner Group and CEO, Homeward Bound.

The notion of life–work balance is an odd one for me. Frankly, I like Hamish's style, what he writes about, his stories and his models. I respect his journey as a leader. But such a lad!

What do I mean? I think privilege is often blind to privilege. So, with love, I offer these thoughts, not to contradict this chapter, but to add to it and include the voice of women leaders, which our planet so sorely needs.

I have worked with thousands of leaders over the years and indeed hundreds of leaders on boards and in executive teams. There was a turning point in my journey, and my company's journey, about 15 years ago when I lifted my head from the feeding bin to realise how consistently (perniciously) women were absent from the executive and board environment.

As I looked around, the few women I met had two faces: one in the predominantly male-led teams they worked in, and another, when they were on their own together. The first was a conforming face, a face that worked to fit in; the second was a connected and collaborative face, expressing a different perspective on the world.

It is this face that I will share here, in a book that offers insight and wisdom to leaders from a very good corporate leader.

Work–life balance, or life–work balance is, I suspect, a metaphor that inspires anxiety in men and often no small amount of frustration and possibly anger in women. (Not sure our author has nailed this yet!) Seventy-five per cent of domestic work is still carried by women. Most very senior corporate leaders (men) have a partner at home managing the 'life' component of 'life–work balance'. For these women, it's not about what they eat or when they exercise (though both are important), it's about food in the fridge, kids to and from school, animals to the vet, friends, parents AND, if they are determined, their work. Women in this context often take a back seat to their successful and loved partner. For women, they find themselves just 'doing'.

Sometimes they also start resenting: their husbands, their kids, their pets, their life. 'Where am I in this journey?' 'Who am I?' They love the whole, and (more often than not) deeply respect their partners. But life balance is not easily won.

For women who have made the alternative choice, to pursue a career, especially one in the corporate sector, a whole other range of challenges emerges in the pursuit of life–work balance. For many, it boils down to choosing not to have kids, or to have them much later in life (IVF territory). They have female friends who have tried to do both and are struggling with the sheer volume of activity they have chosen to do (noting most don't initially see their lives as filled with choice).

So, I would add to this important chapter that balancing and juggling for women represents a deep-seated worry that they are aiming for balance (but don't have it yet) and feel like they have too many balls in the air. Sooner or later something gets dropped.

What's the answer (for men and women) in this space? To get clear on the 'why' of our choices. I would say that mostly, when life–work balance is a challenge, we are simply doing too much and we have to ask ourselves: why?

Chapter 12

What Would Margaret Thatcher say?

Former British Prime Minister Margaret Hilda Thatcher.

In my mind, one of the most legendary conviction leaders of all time. When she died on 8 April 2013, the British population was completely divided. Despite living half my adult life in or near the UK, I was taken aback at the level of polarisation.

A leader of conviction often needs to be black and white. One position or the other, but seldom both. As you will hear, I love conviction leadership and I am inspired by it. I just feel some ideas need compromise and balance.

Being respected *and* liked as a leader: now that's worth chasing.

THE MESSAGE ···························

One of the most common lessons drummed into us throughout our careers is that of earning the respect of others, and that respect is far more important than being liked. Every manager, coach, consultant, textbook and excruciating three-full-day leadership course tells exactly the same story.

It makes perfect sense. Margaret Thatcher said so; my dad even used to say it. So it must be true.

I have a question, though: Does it need to be?

The value of respect is a given. Yet why can't we be respected and liked at the same time? Why do we see this as reserved for a few lucky souls or the ultimate relationship builders, and not as achievable by every leader who walks this planet?

The value of being both respected and liked is clear. People will do what is asked of a leader they respect; but people will walk over coals for a leader they respect *and* like. And as we all know, coals are bloody hot.

···

I always liked Margaret Thatcher. Big call. I have many friends who live in the north of England who will disown me for saying this. (In fact, disown me for even thinking this.)

But the reason why I liked Margaret Thatcher is anything but political. I liked her for her conviction: unwavering, unquestionable and unflappable conviction. I label this as being a 'conviction politician' or a 'conviction leader'. Rightly or wrongly, she gave the perception that she knew more about a topic than anyone else. She would claim that her solution, her direction and her plans were 100 per cent right. I like that conviction. Just show me the way and I will blindly follow. Maybe?

I raise this because seven years ago, I read an article from the *Harvard Business Review*. It paraphrased her on the topic of leadership:

> If you just set out to be liked, you would be prepared to compromise on anything at any time, and you would achieve nothing ... in order to make difficult but necessary decisions for the benefit of the business, it will not always be possible or necessary to be liked.

And I get all that. I truly do. Many times throughout my career I have had to make challenging decisions that have had negative impacts on others. Factory closures, location moves, organisational revamps, downsizing programs, cost-cutting initiatives and, invariably, redundancies. Regardless of the long-term benefits of these decisions, it still hurts to make them. I am told by most coaches that making such calls is just part of doing business and that it should never be taken personally. My belief is different. The day you do not feel personal pain and personal hurt when making decisions that have an adverse impact on others is the day you have been in business too long. If it does not occupy your mind, tie your stomach in knots and make you agonise time and time again over the decision itself, then you are not a true leader of others. You're just a manager paid to do your job.

A word of advice

Implementing a company restructure is a difficult proposition. Two areas of importance:

1. If you need to make a structural change, be decisive about it. Do it early and do everything in your power to do it in one go. There is nothing worse than organisational design changes that move continually from one wave to another. It deflates, demoralises and distracts. Equally, it makes leaders and leadership teams look out of their depth, with limited control over the business.

2. Look after any departing personnel. I will not talk about care, consideration or respect; in my book, they're a given. I will, however, impart one piece of advice that I was given early on in my career: how you treat those who leave matters to those who stay. It took me a while to appreciate this was not just sound business practice, it's mutual compassion for all involved. Thank you, Andy.

Back to Margaret.

She was not alone in her leadership philosophy. My dad used to regularly tell us boys (I have two brothers — older, wiser, but slower around the rugby field) that, in his day, there was a new line drawn when one moved from being a salesperson to a sales manager.

This line was needed for success: when a salesperson was promoted, the once 'mate among mates' employee had no choice but to change in order to meet new responsibilities. And this new level of responsibility required a different persona. Friendship was placed on hold and the new game was about earning all-important respect.

My old man was the kindest, most caring and supportive person that I have ever met. He was also regarded as an exceptional leader who was open to change. In this case, I just reckon that's what his father, his manager and those before them, had told each other.

THE VALUE OF BEING LIKED

Conviction theory aside — which I still love by the way — I just could not fully endorse what Thatcher and so many populist theorists say. Especially her closing line of it not being necessary to be liked. Something didn't gel with me. Was it possible that my Lancastrian friends were right about Maggie?

It got me thinking. Throughout my career, who are those leaders that I have 'stepped over hot coals' to serve?

You know, the additional hours, the compounding pressures, the extra risks, the beyond-the-norm projects that you never once question, you just do. Who have I supported way beyond what is expected of me and definitely beyond my job description and my pay band? Not because of my own personal ambition, but because I was doing it for my leader?

More importantly, why?

The answer was instant and obvious. It was those leaders who I genuinely liked.

Respect is a given and should not be up for debate; I look at it as a point of entry for all leaders. It's hard to achieve, but still simply a point of entry. If you don't have it, success will be mighty tough and nigh-on impossible in the long term. But when I talk about going that extra mile for someone, of giving that extra 30 per cent that most of us have not yet unleashed, respect alone is not enough.

THE SCIENCE OF LIKEABILITY

Before we go any further, let's just pause.

Even as I write this chapter, I know for many readers there will be an underlying discomfort. It probably goes like this: 'When it comes down to getting results, I have no choice but to ignore likeability. There's a reason nice guys finish last.'

As someone who does not rate too highly on the 'feeling' dimension of Myers–Briggs profiling, I hear you. But consider some of the growing scientific research on the subject of leadership likeability.

According to the *Journal of Applied Psychology*, research has found that a manager's likeability has a marked positive effect on how their subordinates and teams rate them on various leadership competencies — including transformational leadership. It found that teams who like their leaders:

- are happier at work

- go above and beyond what is required of them

- experience greater wellbeing

- perform at higher levels.

Although Gallup's engagement dimensions are not directly linked to likeability, we equally know that employee satisfaction and happiness result in increased productivity. Interestingly, many of the characteristics that make up a good leader — including purpose, integrity, authenticity, caring, humour and clarity — are also the same traits that make a likeable human being.

I appreciate it's not black or white, yet from both a personal and business productivity perspective, it makes perfect sense.

Aside

Back when I was heading up Wrigley Pacific, I appointed a very experienced HR director who was driven and unbelievably direct. From the day he joined, Aaron pulled me aside and asked what two things I wished to be known for. I rattled off five. He demanded two. I eventually conceded — growth and engagement. His commitment from that day forth was to do everything he could to ensure I was successful in both. He also held me to account on both of them. So much so, it felt as though he was actually my boss. This accountability was exactly the reason why I hired him and rated him so highly.

Anyway, apart from a great lesson in ruthless focus, I also learned something pertaining to engagement. Every year, I had placed massive effort on ensuring that not only my direct team, but also the entire business, had a 'red hot go' at engagement. Directly due to some amazing line managers around me, I have always had strong engagement scores — for my direct teams and also the business in totality.

My real learning, however, came many years later as it became obvious to me that it is ridiculously easy to get your subordinates to like you.

If your direct reports do not get on with you, who do you think gets hurt the most? Not the boss, that's for sure. If a boss and their subordinate don't get along, there is a high probability that subordinate will miss the promotion, the big salary increase, the freedom and autonomy, and the commitment from their boss to make them the very best that they can be.

This is so obvious, yet it took me an age to realise. Since discovery, my focus has moved significantly. It's no longer about getting the team to like me; rather, it's about getting the team to love each other. Peer-to-peer relationships are paramount for organisational success, and it requires a different lens to make that a reality. When peers respect and like each other (and I feel this is exactly the same for leaders and subordinates by the way), the benefits of feedback are greatly amplified. When someone truly cares for that individual and feels deeply accountable for their ongoing growth and success, they will give open and honest feedback that will land. This alone is significant.

NO DICKHEADS

Does this mean that as a leader you should set out to win a popularity contest? Not at all. If you are liked and not respected, you will fail as a leader. We all know the downfalls of this: avoidance of tough conversations and inertia over difficult decisions are two prime examples.

Yet, why not be a leader who genuinely wants to get on with people on a personal level? Outside of work, do we want to be liked by most of the people we interact with? I think so. If I had to hang around people outside of work who didn't like me, or I didn't like them, then that would be depressing. Life is way too short for that type of drama. Even in Maslow's hierarchy, interpersonal belonging of affiliation, acceptance and affection come just after the fulfilment of physiological and safety needs. So why should work be any different?

My beloved All Blacks live and breathe their 'no dickheads' policy. Regardless of how talented or gifted you are, if you are a dickhead and everyone thinks it, then there is no place for you in our team. Countless sporting teams follow this mantra and, not surprisingly, they are consistently the most successful. Sir Alex Ferguson (widely regarded as Manchester United's greatest ever football manager) continually quoted that a 'championship team will always beat a team of champions'. Yes, I know this is more team unity versus individual, but you get the parallels.

In regard to practical tips for this concept, I've only got a few. I am far from qualified to give you a step-by-step guide as to how to be liked. A coach or a self-help book may assist, yet I doubt it. Success and mastery will come from your own formula and one that works in parallel with your own values and your own persona. Just be authentic when you go about doing it, as there is nothing worse than chasing mateship with ulterior motives. Even the person with a blindfold will see through you.

THE PRACTICAL PART

Chasing 'respected *and* liked'

I use the following framework (see figure 12.1) as a good reminder of what true love leadership looks like.

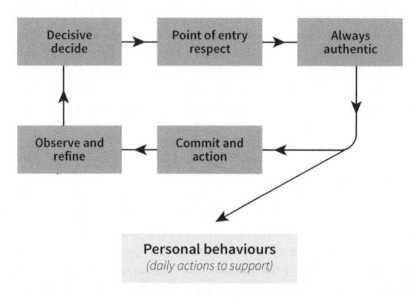

Figure 12.1: love leadership — respected and liked

- **Decide.** Do you want to accept the premise of being respected and liked as a leader? It's okay if you don't; you'll be far from alone. Regardless of what you decide, just make a call and be decisive about it.

- **Respect.** Never lose your focus on earning respect. It is a point of entry and remains the true cornerstone of leadership success.

- **Be authentic.** Being liked or striving to be liked is not about a 'cookie-cutter' approach. Explore what you like in other leaders and seek feedback as to what is liked by others in you. Make these your leadership foundations and daily personal behaviours. In chapter 1, Law, logic, and relationships, I mention those behaviours that assist me in fostering positive working relationships. Use these as thought starters only.

- **Commit.** Both time and energy. Respect is earned and often derived from everyday business operations. Developing friendship is not business as usual and will require considerable effort to make a reality. Planning and thinking are one thing; repeatable observed daily behaviours are another.

- **Observe.** Track the outcomes and refine where needed. When times are challenging and extraordinary effort is required, who steps up to support you? In my experience, when respect and friendship unite, outcomes move from solid to sensational.

If you genuinely chase respect and likeability, and by chance you don't observe any behavioural change in others, don't stress and do not give up. Just ask if you feel happier as a person if you are liked as well as respected. I strongly suspect you will answer yes.

If not, maybe a life in British politics could be your answer.

THE CRITIQUE

A brief review from Ashok Vasudevan, entrepreneur, impact adviser and academician, co-founder and chair of Tasty Bite and CEO for the Centre for the Spread of Affordable Wellness, Singapore.

••

'To be liked and respected' cannot become the purpose of a leader. They are the consequence of their actions.

Perhaps the most widely acclaimed theory of leadership is the Blake and Mouton grid, from the 1960s. It described leaders in two dimensions: task-oriented and people-oriented. A '9.1' leader is 9 on tasks and a mere 1 on people — basically, an authoritarian. While the '1.9' boss is full of bonhomie and less demanding. A perfect 9.9 score is the aspiration.

It's tempting to think of leaders in terms of styles and behaviours. We describe them with nouns (CEO, president, chairman, general manager) and adjectives (likeable, impressive, inspiring, aggressive). The underlying belief is that by emulating their traits (adjectives) we will gain their titles (nouns). That is a bit simplistic. My friend Hamish Thomson brings the struggle out explicitly in this chapter: 'conviction leader' is the perfect example of this adjective–noun syndrome.

I'd rather think of leadership in terms of impact and outcomes. Or, to use another part of speech, in terms of verbs. Instead of styles of effective leadership we read in self-help books, let me propose five verbs of leadership:

1. Leaders don't just emerge. They *evolve*. Good leaders are continuous learners who periodically come up with new tricks. Ratan Tata evolved from an uninspired run at failed NELCO in the 1970s to Chairman of Tata Sons, transforming it into one of the most respected global conglomerates.

2. They may or may not appear to be mavericks, but good leaders *change the rules*. As author James Carse writes in his book *Finite and Infinite Games*, 'Finite players play within boundaries: infinite players play with boundaries.' Silicon Valley entrepreneurs almost make a habit of changing the rules. Apple, Amazon, Airbnb, Uber and Facebook are making it impossible to even define which industries they are in!

3. Good leaders are not always inspiring. They *seek inspiration*. Leadership is really about followership. We are often told to hire people smarter than us. Truth be told, they are there the whole time. We just don't see them. But when we do, results are magical. We meet aspirations and inspire performance. Good leaders will walk on coals for their team, not the other way around.

4. Leaders don't just imagine a future. They *help create it*. Elon Musk literally dragged Detroit to Silicon Valley with Tesla. Is it a car with no cylinders and pistons or a computer on wheels? Painting a future helps coalesce the team and unleashes imagination. Creating a future is the outcome

5. Finally, leaders *define purpose* — not activity. MBA is not an acronym for 'manage by activity'. Our penchant for staying busy drives our schedules and defines our style. But 'managing by purpose' helps free up organisation time by eliminating pointless activities. Understanding why we do what we do is a powerful motivator.

Chapter 13

Bring On the Grilling

I don't know about you, but I am always amazed at the breadth of qualities and attributes possessed by others.

Dōgen Zenji was a Japanese Buddhist, priest, writer, poet, philosopher and founder of the School of Zen back in the 1200s. As a Zen Master, he was also one of the first to promote the practice of *zazen* — sitting meditation.

What appeals to me is his outlook on lessons derived from harsh truth and realities. As he said, 'We must always be disturbed by the truth'.

We can gain insight from anywhere, and exceptional leaders will know where to find it.

Even if it's painful to do so.

THE MESSAGE ·······················

We all dislike being told off. It restricts our perceived levels of freedom, and although this sounds somewhat childlike, the older we get, the more it seems to piss us off. (If this is just me, then maybe you should skip this chapter.)

I know of no ideal way to handle being told off. At any age.

Do I push back? Should I question and challenge authority? Possibly argue with attitude? Could I play the victim card or go after the sympathy vote? Or maybe I just take it, let my eyes tear up and hope like hell it stops quickly. I imagine it depends on the situation and who's involved, but to be honest, I have little clue. This doesn't bother me, though.

What I do know is that many benefits come from getting a serve. (A grilling, roasting, scorching or whatever you want to call it.) There is always a golden nugget that comes from it. I'm not talking the 'bad boss' principle that we cover in chapter 8. It's the insight behind the grilling that I'm fascinated with. Seldom is it about the content itself; the context holds the key. Always the context.

So listen to the grilling and take it all in. Cry, push back, challenge, slam the door, hurl abuse or do whatever takes your fancy. Your call entirely. But, as it is unfolding, I want you to muster every ounce of energy you have and look for the real insight involved. Most times, it will be gold.

···

Ever heard of the word 'reactance'? (I hadn't but then again, that does not surprise me. I find new words and meanings fascinating, yet seldom can I remember them, let alone pronounce them. Despite this, I have always thought I would be a reasonable sports commentator, tennis in particular. It is uncanny how every year during the Australian Open, I raise insightful commentary in front of the family TV, only to hear Jim Courier or Lleyton Hewitt repeat it a few seconds later. It is a skill set that will take me nowhere and unfortunately, my pronunciation of any Eastern European tennis player's name is dismal to say the least.) Back to reactance.

THEORY OF REACTANCE

In 1966, psychologist Jack Brehm introduced his theory of reactance. He stated that people react strongly when their freedom is being threatened or restricted. Specifically, they had an 'unpleasant motivational arousal' (his words, not mine) to offers, persons, rules or regulations that threaten or eliminate specific behavioural freedoms, and the larger the threat to freedom, the larger the resistance to it.

Ever since hearing this theory, I have taken a real interest in it. With autonomy and freedom being two of my most important values, the theory makes perfect sense to me. In my early career, I used to regularly push back and challenge authority. At the time, I always assumed this was due to my age, yet maybe it was a little deeper than that.

The interesting part is that for some bizarre reason, I do not mind getting a grilling. It seems odd, but I find getting served or told off keeps things really interesting. I definitely do not seek them out, and, when they do happen, like most others, I get upset, frustrated and even angry. And yet, after a relatively short passage of time, the grillings just become fascinating stories and great reflection points.

The other reason for enjoying them — and hopefully a slightly more compelling one — is that over the years, I have noticed that after every serve of note, I seem to get better. It doesn't happen in the moment, and I don't have a sudden epiphany when waking up the next morning. Yet, over time, I just start to get it. No matter how unjustified or even abhorrent I think the grilling was, there is always a hidden gem contained within the message and the way that it is delivered. The *why* it was delivered and the *way* it was delivered is the context that makes these serves invaluable. Let me give you a few examples.

SAMSON FIRES UP THE GRILL

One of my most beloved bosses over the years was a chap called Samson, then President of Wrigley Asia Pacific. He, along with his legendary predecessor, Michael, had built a multibillion-dollar gum, mints and sugar confections business within China in less than 10 years. They had more distribution points across the country than Coca-Cola. As Samson would elegantly explain to all international visitors, 'It's easier for one to ride a push bike to the top of the Great Wall with a month's supply of gum on their back than half a day's stock of that brown fizzy liquid.'

Anyway, one thing that both Michael and Samson had instilled within their leadership teams, and indeed, their entire associate base, was loyalty. Undivided loyalty. It made Robert De Niro's 'circle of trust' look tame by comparison.

One case in point was when I had a visit from the company owners. At the time I was based in Sydney and was the CEO/Managing Director for Wrigley Pacific. The Mars family had just acquired the Wrigley business, which still to this day is referred to by Warren Buffett as one of the most successful acquisitions and mergers of recent time. (This is saying something, as the purchase price was approximately US$23 billion and took place only months before the stock market crash of late 2008.) A massive credit to all involved.

I have always had a good relationship with the Mars family. Their passion and commitment to the business is second to none, and I feel privileged to have worked for so long in such a purpose- and values-led company. This is not to say that I have not been on the receiving end of some very direct and very confrontational dressing-down moments. Those, however, are private stories for another day! At the end of this particular factory tour, I was asked a simple and direct question: 'What do you want to happen, Hamish?' It pertained directly to the future of the Australian Wrigley gum factory. This was the time of the Asian 'super-factory' alternatives, which on paper, always looked compelling.

My response was instant: 'We want to move mints production from China to Australia. We need to control production and lead innovation alongside being more flexible in meeting domestic demand. We have just taken market leadership, volume is exploding and will continue to explode. What's more, we want to pave the way for a sustainable and more scale-efficient Australian factory that will support at least a generation of associates to follow.'

It was literally a 30-second response that came out within a nanosecond of being asked. As a local leadership team, we were 100 per cent pre-aligned to this message and, when requested, it was an easy line to deliver.

Now, I cannot recall exactly the date and time of this meeting, but for the sake of the story, let's say it took place on Wednesday evening at 6 pm.

That night, I thought nothing more of it.

At 10 the next morning, I received a call from Samson's executive assistant, Crystal: 'Samson would like to see you in person, 8 am tomorrow, Hong Kong office.' Based on her tone, there was no point in asking for further clarification: none was offered, nor would any be forthcoming. Even following calls to my peers in the Asia Pacific leadership team, total radio silence.

Ten hours later I was in Hong Kong and at 7.58 the next morning, I walked into the top floor of the iconic Bank of China building and into Samson's office. In those days, Samson was old-school Wrigley—he still had the typically large, posh corporate office.

He was seated at his desk and standing to his right was a good friend and peer of mine, Samuel. At the time, Sam was VP of Asia Pacific Supply. He had his head down. Not a good sign.

I went first: 'Good morning, gentlemen,' and reached out to shake hands. No response. Nothing.

To place this in context, Samson remains one of my all-time favourite bosses. Super supportive and genuinely friendly to myself, my wife and family and my entire domestic team. Unquestionably, he was an inspirational leader whom I admired and continue to admire very much. Admiration aside, it was clear I was not there for small talk.

For the next five minutes, no more but definitely no less, Samson talked of one thing only: team. The importance of trust and the importance of closeness versus all those who sit outside your direct team. Why trust and confidence in a team is so vital and how damaging it can be when one breaks it. He recited historical examples dating back to the 16 ruling emperors of the Ming dynasty, which he illustrated with the colourful consequences that resulted when one went outside the inner sanctum.

Interestingly, not once did he mention the Mars family meeting that I'd had less than 48 hours before. Not once. It was crystal clear, though, that I had raised sensitive issues outside of his direct team. I was reminded with total clarity that I was very much a part of the Asia Pacific Leadership team and as such, there were clear expectations that I needed to follow. This included the hierarchy and timing of when you discuss and finalise sensitive issues (i.e., always with your direct team first before anyone else!).

Interestingly, about three minutes into the lecture, I did consider pushing back. 'Hang on a moment,' I thought, 'I was asked a very simple question by the company owners and I responded with exactly the same requests and discussions that we have had multiple times in person — with you and with the wider leadership team.' Yes, my amygdala was pretty active, yet I said absolutely nothing. I had total respect for Samson and, although it was very clear that I was on the end of a dressing down, it was done with pure class, clarity and conviction, delivered with total respect, and never once diverged into a personal attack.

At the end of the meeting — I had travelled a long way for five minutes — I will always remember what happened next. Samson stood up, walked over to me, placed his arm around my shoulder, walked me to the door and simply said: 'Don't worry, we are family and you will have my full support.'

Nothing else was said, or ever mentioned again by Samson. I did not need to regain his level of trust. As far as he was concerned, I had not lost it. To me, this is what great leadership is about.

It probably took me a full year to appreciate the context of that meeting. I seldom think of the content (the production line in question moved to Australia and is still going strong today), but I think with regularity around the lessons derived. Team alignment and 'First Team' mentality have since become cornerstones of my own leadership style. Equally, respectful leadership when delivering crucial conversations remains paramount. Thank you, Samson. I now watch *Meet the Fockers* and the circle of trust with a whole new level of understanding!

A word of advice

The Five Dysfunctions of a Team by Patrick Lencioni is an exceptional read and I feel a must for all leadership teams, with clear insight relating to 'First Team' mentality and total team alignment. Best of all, it's short, concise and definitely one you can finish.

THE BRITISH GRILLMASTER

As it goes, not all serves are delivered in the same respectful manner. Probably my harshest work grilling was my first ever received.

It was 1991. I was working in the London advertising scene and after being quietly moved on from my original copywriting duties — to the benefit of the agency and also the entire print-viewing British population — I started activities as a young account executive. Being fresh-faced and insanely curious, I began frequenting numerous 'free to attend' industry speaking engagements. One in particular was hosted by the infamous Scottish journalist and broadcaster Andrew Neil, then editor of *The Sunday Times* (part of Rupert Murdoch's News Corporation). Andrew also happened to be the largest client of the advertising agency I was working for.

Looking around the large conference room that evening, I noticed that I was the only one from the agency in attendance. After all, it was an outside-work event and, importantly for me, it was free entry that included unlimited food and drink. I liked these events.

Andrew talked about the changing landscape of the British newspaper and communications industry and repeatedly referenced the likely impact on those who advertise within it. Looking back now, how correct he was. I won't go into the details, but being the young and energetic Antipodean that I was — and remember, I was up against very well-educated and well-versed Eton and Oxford graduates at the time — I promptly raced back to the office and put together a three-page summary document outlining the key points raised, potential implications for the industry and possible courses of action for the agency.

Yes, I had discovered something that would change the world of advertising forever! Bright and early the next morning, I placed a hard copy on each of the directors' desks and, like a good black labrador puppy, I sat back and waited for the praise to come rolling in.

I had one early bite.

I was called into the office of one of the senior agency directors. Paul was probably in his mid to late forties at the time. Short, balding and a little chubby, he headed up the profitable and super important media department. (I normally wouldn't call someone chubby, but as it turned out, we didn't end up being great friends.) He was about number four within the agency hierarchy, with a reputation as a fierce, no-nonsense negotiator. He was very good at his job.

If my meeting with Samson lasted five minutes, this one lasted two.

I managed to open his office door about halfway when the torrent of abuse started. 'Who the fuck do you think you are, you little Australian wanker?' (This was not the time to tell him that I was actually from New Zealand.) 'How dare you come in here and write this shit and even consider that your opinion means jack? You are not paid to give your uneducated and unrated opinions to anyone. So, fuck off.'

Look, I'm probably paraphrasing a bit as it was a long time ago. Either way, it was colourful language and it was not pretty. As mentioned, he was not a big guy, but when you are only 21 and some head honcho is standing over you and yelling directly in your face with half the office outside listening to every word, it's not a good situation. I admit it, my eyes started to well up.

After two minutes, I snapped.

In my mind, if I deserve a serve then I am more than okay to take it. We all make mistakes, and part of the learning process itself is just having to accept the negative consequences. When a serve is not justified, though, something rises inside me and I just cannot help myself. In this case, I don't believe it was warranted — and definitely not to the levels that he was dishing out.

I will not pretend that I had a Clint Eastwood–type moment and remember every stoic line that I said back to Paul. I didn't swear, though, nor did I raise my voice. I do recall telling him I was sorry if it offended him and that it had not been my intention to do so. I also told him I didn't appreciate the way he was speaking to me and suggested that he should stop doing it and should stop now. As it transpired, this last bit didn't go down well with Paul, so it was no surprise that when I left his office, the tirade still continued.

Over the next 24 hours I waited anxiously for my boss to call me in and hand me my exit ticket back home to New Zealand. Potentially a free flight, but at the time, I was not thinking that positively.

As it happened, the next day I bumped into the CEO and chair of the agency. Peter was like a god in the agency, and every aspiring account executive was in awe of him. The irony was that he was so revered that none of the young folk ever dared to talk to him. (For reference, Peter had the biggest Mercedes S-Class that I had ever seen, along with a personal 24-hour chauffeur called Arthur. I kid you not: Arthur.)

It so happened that when I first started at the agency, one of my many jobs was to stock the bar fridges in each of the directors' offices. Peter's office was no exception. Italian Soave is still engrained on my mind as his regular lunchtime tipple. One morning I saw that poking out of his sports bag was a badminton racket. Upon enquiring, he informed me that for the past two years, he had been having weekly lessons with a legendary professional coach from Korea. When he asked if I played, I cheekily — and honestly — said no, but that I was a pretty handy tennis player, so I would fancy my chances if he wanted a game.

Remember the chapter on law, logic and relationships?

Well, from then on, every few weeks I would join Peter and Arthur in the S-Class Merc and we would go off to play badminton. (For the record: our first match and my first ever game of badminton ended in a thrashing. Something like 18-1, 18-0, 18-2. I recall calling my dad that night, telling him I had to virtually give Peter those three points. He was not a natural.)

Back to the grilling. When I saw Peter later that day, I sheepishly mentioned that my memo had not gone down well with Paul and that I hoped that it did not cause any unnecessary disruption or tension within the agency. Peter stopped, turned to me and said calmly, 'No idea why he felt like that, I thought it was pretty clear and well written. That's just Paul for you.' Nothing else was said, and he turned and walked away. Never underestimate the power of relationships.

I took a lot out of that grilling. Not content wise, but definitely context. I repeatedly asked myself, why did he lose the plot so badly? He certainly didn't feel threatened by me, and my report was not exactly revolutionary or even that controversial. So why the reaction? Or was it just me who brought out the worst in others?

The answer came to me years later when the former Global President of Mars Incorporated spoke at a senior leader's conference in Washington, DC. He said that he seldom listened to the content of what most people would say to him — because invariably, he knew what they were going to say along with the likely answer. (He was not short of confidence.) Rather, he would just listen and observe their emotion. Why were they so passionate or heated on a particular subject? Why so indifferent, reserved or even removed from another?

Essentially, he was bypassing the content and focusing on the context. This is so simple, yet so very powerful. From that day forward I have learned to watch someone's emotion more than their messaging. Context over content.

In regard to my agency grilling, knowing the context helped explain a lot. At the time, there was considerable pressure on media billings for the business. Indeed, some of the movements in client spending that Andrew Neil had talked of had already started unfolding and had begun to affect the agency. It wasn't massive or crippling, yet it was enough to place additional internal pressure and scrutiny on Paul and his team.

Either that, or maybe he was just having a bad day!

THE PRACTICAL PART

How to benefit from a grilling

Please don't overthink this concept. When you do get served, don't be left perplexed about the situation; rather, make sure that you get true insight, meaning and benefits through following the steps outlined in figure 13.1.

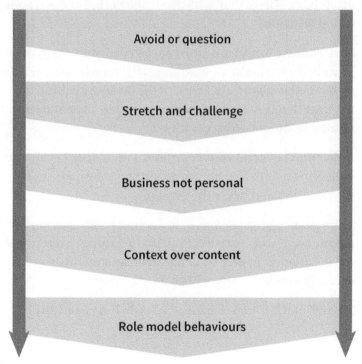

The Five Steps to Insight

- Avoid or question
- Stretch and challenge
- Business not personal
- Context over content
- Role model behaviours

Figure 13.1: bring on the grilling

- **Avoid.** Do your best to not get grilled in the first place. If you have had too many incidents of note, then maybe you need to ask yourself two questions: 'Is it me? Why is it me?' I have repeatedly had to do this over my career.

- **Stretch.** Conversely, if you are not getting any serves at all, then you need to ask yourself a harder question. 'Am I pushing hard enough?'

  Do not just gloss over this. If you are not stretching and challenging yourself enough, you are not doing justice to your untapped abilities that benefit both yourself and the organisation.

- **De-personalise.** Where warranted and despite the pain it may cause, fully accept the grilling itself. Ignore the manner in which it is being delivered and try not to take it personally. We all screw up at times — if we didn't, life would be boring and little progress would be made.

- **Seek context.** Look for context ahead of content. Sometimes there will be necessary messaging that you will need to adhere to, but in the majority of cases it's the meaning behind the message that is important. Search and seek it out and remain insatiably curious along the way.

- **Role model crucial conversations.** I'm talking here about delivering a roasting, not receiving one. Always be hard on the situation and never the person.

  Additionally, always explain the context and emotion behind the message you are delivering. It's one thing to tell someone off; it's another to give someone a life lesson. If you are an exceptional leader, you will go for the latter.

  Finally, and without debate, always do it respectfully.

MODELS FOR THE WHITEBOARD

Situational Leadership

There are loads of books and models on having crucial conversations. I have used many, yet I always come back to the simplest (see figure 13.2). The Situational Leadership Model (SLM) was first developed in the mid 1970s by Ken Blanchard and Paul Hersey. It allows flexibility in style and approach when giving feedback. It's particularly relevant when you have a hard message to deliver (for example, sometimes you will need to just say it as it is with little coaching support along the way — a position of S1 — Directive). Equally, it can be very useful in understanding the context when you are on the receiving end of a grilling.

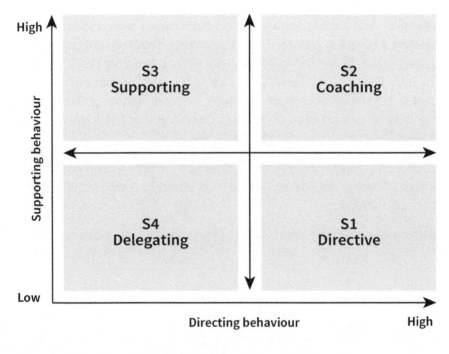

Figure 13.2: situational leadership — Blanchard model

Feedback Effectiveness

There is an art to giving feedback, and seldom is it followed. During coaching sessions, I frequently use this model (see figure 13.3). Despite what we are told, the best feedback is when fact is combined with emotion. When linked, it is relatable, compelling and importantly, makes a difference.

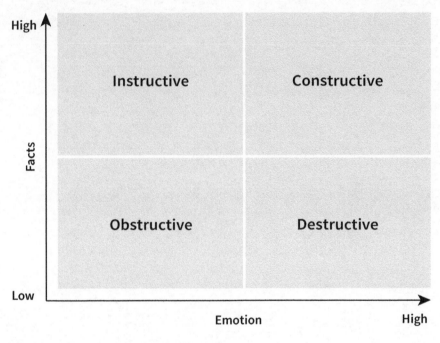

Figure 13.3: types of feedback effectiveness

THE CRITIQUE

A brief review from award-winning growth and transformation technology leader (former Slingshot CEO & Spotify MD), food & travel journalist, Karen Lawson.

....

Whether it's about not having enough sex, who has done the dishes or not meeting a deadline, there is conflict everywhere. We are constantly getting a dressing down from work, home, family, friends. It's part of the fabric of life.

The real difference here is trust and intent. When you have those two things, feedback and roasting can be powerful motivators for change. Without them, it can be a disaster. I must quote Diane Smith-Gander, who really made me laugh with her comment around feedback: 'Keep it, throw it away or re-gift it.' It's stayed with me — how empowering.

The ratio of good to bad feedback in order to create a happy environment is 5 to 1. It's a good reminder for us all of the role we play and the damage we can do. I think some people's ratios are a little different; some people seem to be Teflon-like in their ability to shrug things off, while I and others absorb every word in a desire to be a better person and leader. As leaders, with positions of power, we really should know better and be thoughtful in how we distribute feedback.

I have learned through leadership roles — which have spanned global corporates, joint ventures, venture capital and start-ups — the value of understanding our superpowers and how other people appreciate them.

Case in point: I was a young female in a male-dominated industry (telcos in the UK). My sales numbers were the best in the country and I absolutely loved my job. My customers, who I went to the ends of the earth for, loved me back. I had a new boss.

'I have heard a lot about you, Karen', was followed by an expletive-filled tirade about 'average performance'. Through belief in my abilities and knowledge of my results, I pushed back. He smirked and responded with, 'Good, I was just testing you.' What a dick! He supported me simply because of my success. I was established, had my power base and connections. If I had been new within my role, he would have crushed me, and I really think he would have delighted in it. People in positions of power should know better.

Speaking of context, if you are in the start-up world, getting a roasting is awesome — it means 'Hey, someone actually saw me and cared enough to give feedback!' Getting a roasting and failing are generally rites of passage that are great learning opportunities. Start-ups embrace failure; they grow from it. It's what makes them strong. If you are not failing, then you're not pushing the boundaries enough. In the corporate world, it's different. Sometimes those 'flearnings' (failure/learnings) can be done from head office, but seldom locally. A miss.

Always think about that 5 to 1 ratio. If you care, you have the right to roast. If not, perhaps the work that should be done is with the person serving it, not the other way around.

Chapter 14

The Hardest Part of a Decision

Sandra Day O'Connor was the first woman to serve on the Supreme Court of the United States. She was appointed by President Ronald Reagan in 1981 and served until her retirement in 2006. A moderate conservative, she was known for her dispassionate and meticulously researched opinions.

Can you only imagine the type of pressure and intense scrutiny she would have faced on a daily basis?

Decisions of historical precedence. Decisions of national, often global, significance. Decisions with political ramifications and decisions of public transparency.

Apparently, she was exceptional.

Why is it some people can handle the pressures of decision making so much better than others? Why do the majority ruminate, deliberate, agonise and personalise?

The hardest part of a decision is the decision itself.

THE MESSAGE ·······················

As human beings, we tend to be pretty harsh on ourselves. If we are not questioning growth and progress, then we are pondering happiness and contentment levels. Invariably, we start thinking of the past: ruminations on what was and what could have been.

Decision making is something of an oddity. Although we make thousands of decisions every day, many of us agonise over them. Literally. They make us second guess ourselves, question our abilities, and, for many, they can lead to heartache and inertia.

···

Big decisions will always need thought and consideration. I don't mind if I have to agonise over making them. Serious upfront anguish is more than okay.

Once a decision is made, however, that should be the end of it. You have done the hard work and made the best call with the information you have. If you have followed a clear decision-making process, the outcome will be what it will be and there is absolutely no reason to second-guess it.

The key to thinking like this comes down to one thing: making sure you have followed the very best decision-making process humanly possible. It must be rigorous and prescriptive. Without it, every decision will be hard.

For 20 years, I have attempted to execute the mantra, 'the hardest part of a decision is the decision itself'. It has saved me a lot of pain and a lot of heartache. Once I have gone through the clear process of decision making, ensuring I stick to guiding principles, I remind myself that, whatever the outcome, it was the best decision at the time. I accept it, endeavour to never question it and I move on.

I never used to think this way. Having spoken to countless leaders, I realised I was not alone.

REFLECTORS VS FORWARD-LOOKERS

Many people in this world are what I term 'reflectors'. These are individuals who need time to reflect on what's gone before. I am a supporter of reflection that leads to clear insight, learning and tangible action. It is invaluable.

I am not, however, supportive of negative reflection: rumination that adds little or no value. Deliberating over a decision that has already been made is a massive hindrance to an organisation. I'm not talking about deliberating over the *process* you used to make that decision. This is critical and is a non-negotiable. In fact, that part of the review should be relentless. No, I'm talking about questioning the decision itself. It helps no-one and is a clear distraction. It affects you personally and, if you are a leader of others, it is a disturbance that your team and organisation can ill afford.

Aside

Rumination refers to the tendency to repetitively think about the causes, situational factors and consequences of one's negative emotional experience. Overwhelming self-criticism and negative self-talk about one's failures and shortcomings are common. Most of these continuous thoughts tend to be sad or dark. Some medical experts have linked rumination to mental anxiety. They say that the habit can prolong or intensify depression as well as impair one's ability to think and process raw emotions. This can also lead to feelings of isolation, which can in turn push other people away. It can be a very dangerous thing, rumination, so I encourage you to be as positive and forward thinking as possible in your reflections.

Although this decision-making mantra (the hardest part of a decision is the decision itself) works well for me, I need to be transparent. Based on my personality type, it should work.

I look forward and seldom think about the past. Although avoiding negative rumination has been a deliberate change for me, it has also been a relatively easy change to make. While this sits well with me, it can have negative consequences for others; the Gallup Institute would label this future-thinking state an 'unintended or overused skill.' I label it a flaw within my leadership style.

While I view the past as history and simply a learning opportunity, I seldom stay in the moment. I am immediately on to the next chapter. For reflectors, this makes for a very challenging and annoying boss. I often do not allow them time or headspace to reflect. For some people, positive reflection is a critical part of their learning process. Without it, they will never perform at their best next time around. Equally, although I move easily and quickly on to the next challenge, many reflectors need a form of closure before moving on. This is a different psychological style and I need to be cognisant of their needs.

Another downside of my style is what the Buddhist priests have known for thousands of years: 'When you live in the future, you vacate the present.' Fortunately, my strong drive for immediate results keeps me firmly in the moment, but it is a risk I am conscious of (and have even undertaken mindfulness training to counteract).

DECISION-MAKING NON-NEGOTIABLES

Some non-negotiables: if you're thinking that the world of decision making will now be a cruisy affair, I want to impart some reality checks.

Regardless of whether you decide to follow this mantra or not, you are responsible for the decisions that you have made. There's no avoiding it.

From my perspective, these include being fully:

- **answerable for continual improvement in decision making.** You only 'chill out' on a decision if you have sweated (big time) over the process you undertook to make that decision. Ruthless interrogation and analysis of the decision-making process is critical to perpetual improvement. Without it, anguish should remain.

- **accountable for the executional excellence of the decision in question.** Some people distance themselves from this. Not me. If I am the one who has made the decision, then I will be accountable for execution. I may not always carry out the implementation myself, yet I should always be held to account. I admit, there is a degree of personal control being exerted when taking this level of accountability. Good or bad, it has definitely made my original decision making that much more thorough, decisive and pragmatic.

- **responsible for learning from every major decision that I make.** I have a commitment to be transparent and vulnerable as to where and when I have got that process wrong. Sharing insights and learning, especially those that you are not proud of, is a hallmark of authentic leadership.

- **liable for the outcome of the decision itself.** If it was my call, or a call under my appointed team, then the buck stops with me.

Although some will find these levels of responsibility daunting, to me they are what keeps leadership real and undeniably fascinating.

THE PRACTICAL PART

Understanding and applying effective decisions

Although this concept is fairly entrenched in my memory, every now and then I remind myself of the following principles (see figure 14.1). It's not an exhaustive list on decision making; just a practical one.

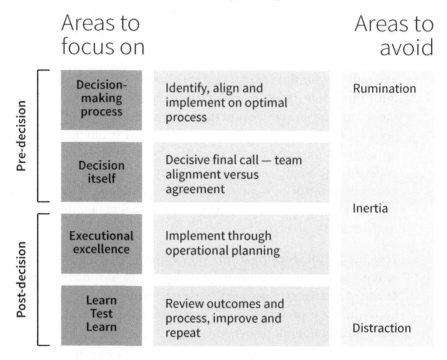

Figure 14.1: decision making — a model for ruminators

The areas to focus on are as follows. (As for areas to avoid, we've talked enough about these. Do your best not to go there!)

Decision-making process

Start with team alignment on what process and model you want to use. There is a plethora to choose from. My only advice is to establish guiding principles up front that will assist you throughout the decision-making process. They are guidelines, boundaries and tolerance levels of what will and will not be acceptable for the decision itself. If I was facing a decision, for instance, of whether to invest in a new manufacturing line locally or secure volume from an offshore factory, I would be including up-front guidelines pertaining to customer service and quality levels, inventory and cash flow positions, corporate reputation and employee engagement impacts, overhead absorption rates, coupled with tolerance levels of resource allocation and change management capabilities, et cetera. Use these guidelines when reviewing alternative options and raise them when you observe emotional bias coming into play from team members.

Secondly, ensure clarity on decision-making rights. I know this sounds elementary, yet I have seen and been involved in too many inefficient examples to not highlight this. (For reference, my 'go to' framework is RAPID from Bain.)

Decision itself

Once you have made the decision, it must have team alignment, not necessarily team agreement. The words sound similar, they are anything but.

Patrick Lencioni details this in his book *The Five Dysfunctions of a Team*. Disagreement on a final team decision is more than okay. Personally, I like this. It gives me added confidence that all viable options have had rigorous debate and necessary tension to deliver the best outcome. Non-alignment after a decision, however, is totally unacceptable.

Once a decision is made, all team members, regardless of whether they're in agreement with it or not, must commit to it and be a line of one. No post-meeting eyebrow raising, hands from the grave, triangulation or whatever you want to call it. Non-alignment will always be the hallmark of substandard teams. Additionally, when you do make the decision, you need to be intentionally decisive. When a decision needs to be made, a 'maybe' helps absolutely no-one.

Execution with excellence

Unless your strategic choice is a shocker, it is usually execution that leads to success or failure.

Learn, test, learn

Learn from old, test the new and repeat. This is why I am passionate around knowledge management and learning documentation.

MODELS FOR THE WHITEBOARD

Past, Present, Future framework—a model to assist reflectors

Three behaviours that I regularly see in leaders — including myself:

- dismissing what has gone before me

- showing disregard and disinterest to those in the midst of daily operational challenges

- portraying an absence of future hope and prosperity.

With this knowledge, when I present to wide and disparate audiences, I use the following framework (see figure 14.2).

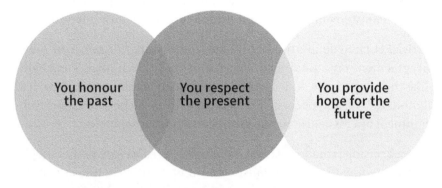

Figure 14.2: honour, respect, hope — a framework for past, present, future

I honour the past, I respect the present and I provide hope for the future. This has saved a lot of emotional discomfort for those around me (particularly reflectors).

Data to Action Conversion model—helping accelerate decision making

I use this model (see figure 14.3) to accelerate effective decision making. It can be threatening as it also demands ultimate accountability.

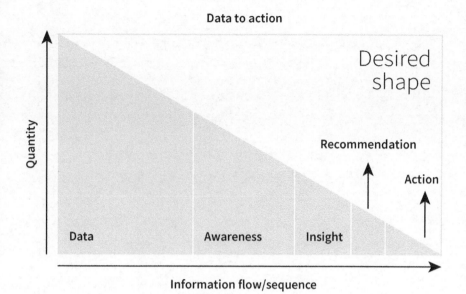

Figure 14.3: data leverage 101

Exceptional businesses and exceptional people take data, disseminate it for awareness, create relevant insight, recommend clear strategic paths and take action. Average organisations and average employees do the opposite. They are overwhelmed by quantity, share the wrong information, are general with insight, absent from recommendation and are void of accountability and action.

The blocks in the model explain the current way of working within most organisations. Heaps of data with very little resulting action.

In my ideal universe, I wish never to hear an insight unless it is fully leveraged. Without conversion it's absolutely meaningless. An exceptional person will show hunger and drive to take a compelling insight, place a clear recommendation and passionately demand full implementation. Like you, I want to be surrounded by exceptional.

A final note: remember, just like a supermarket shelf, too much choice leads to confusion, which leads to customers walking away without making a purchase. Do your best not to make the same mistake with too much data.

THE CRITIQUE

A brief review from one of Asia's most experienced FMCG leaders, Christina Keilthy, Chief Executive Officer, The Strategic Thinking Group, Singapore.

Hard decisions. We have all been through the agony—but the good news is that, over time and with experience, we do get better at it, so there is hope.

We make many decisions every day—what to wear, what to eat, what to put on our 'to-do' lists—but there are some decisions with bigger and more significant impact that we struggle with. Those that involve relationships with family members, the health and wellbeing of our loved ones and the future of our children. At work, the hardest decisions for me have been in three areas: the firing of employees, closing of factories and new job opportunities.

They are the decisions that affect the livelihoods of the people I work with. As a 25-year-old unit manager at Procter & Gamble, I had to terminate the services of a sales representative who committed fraud. Although it was clear he had to be terminated, it did not make the decision any easier. Throughout the investigation process, I was hoping it would turn out to be a false accusation. This was quickly followed by how to conduct the meeting without destroying all the sales representative's confidence in himself. It was demanding.

A second decision was as a GM. I was asked to close a factory in Hong Kong that had employees who had worked in the plant longer than I had been alive. I used the following process—the same one I still use today.

- What's the problem? (Have I verified all facts and figures?)

- What are my options? (Explore each and every one of them.)

- What are the pros and cons of each of my options?

- Make the decision.

- Take responsibility and accept the worst-case consequences.

- Work hard to avoid or minimise the worst-case scenario.

Using this process, I convinced the global team to keep the factory rather than open a new plant in China. I am proud to say that the factory still stands.

Even hard decisions can be rewarding.

Chapter 15
Culture Doesn't Matter

The world can be a fickle place. One moment, you're the toast of the town; the next, a memory on a postcard.

Business can be like that. It's one of the reasons I strive for brands and companies to stay ahead of the curve. It is a magnificent thing when it works.

Culture is similar. You think it's always present, always on and always working. Then just like that, one day it's not. A poor imitation of what it was and what it could have been.

As Coco Chanel said, 'Fashion is made to go out of fashion'. Like fashion, culture evolves.

If not stoked, it flounders.

I forgot this once. Never again.

THE MESSAGE ·

Familiarity breeds contempt. We get used to things being as they are, and this can lead to a sense of entitlement. A culture of entitlement can be a dangerous place, for both an individual and for a business. We perceive unique and valued experiences as business as usual. As a result, we no longer see them as being special. And when we don't see things as being extraordinary, we take them for granted. This is not only hazardous: it is also very wrong. I see culture as falling into this trap.

When you venture into a bad culture, you feel it immediately. The feel of the place penetrates deeply and you either leave or you're sucked into it. When you enter a great culture, the benefits are vast and obvious; they do not need to be explained. The quandary is how to keep that culture — more so, how to evolve it into something even better. Unless it's fuelled on a day-to-day basis, that culture will steadily dwindle.

The problem is that a great culture has a curse: it's exceptionally difficult to evolve.

· ·

I have always enjoyed walking into an outstanding advertising agency.

As soon as you enter the building, there's an infectious buzz that radiates throughout the place. There's always noise — lots of noise. Cool sounds emanate, loud, yet never irritating. People are everywhere, but nobody cares. Some congregate in small groups, others in large herd-like gatherings, and those on their own are talking. Always phone talking. Outrageous, over-the-top hand movements, fits of uncontrolled laughter and sudden outbursts of dismay or bewilderment echo throughout the space. They also seem to be cool cats; young, trendy and energetic. Invariably, one or two are stressed, with their head down, eyes fixated on nothing, but that's okay. They're the exception.

There are pool tables, foosball tables, air hockey tables, dart boards, bean bags, pogo sticks, digital walls, retro coffee machines and bar fridges packed with copious amounts of alcohol, organic smoothies and kale. (Bloody kale.) Every now and then, there is a 'sit down on your arse' space invaders video game. And you want to know the coolest thing of all? Every single one of these ridiculously expensive and over the top artefacts is constantly being used!

Very seldom do I give much thought to what I wear to work. I like fashion, yet I am not fashionable. When I visit an outstanding advertising agency however, I stop and think carefully about what to put on that morning. When I leave the agency, regardless of the meeting content, I feel good. I feel younger (no comments, please), positive, energised, invigorated and definitely have more of a 'fuck yes, I can do anything' type of attitude.

Interesting isn't it? I can get this type of feeling literally radiating through my entire body simply from the vibe of a collective working environment. I don't need a leadership course, inspirational speech or self-help motivational book. I just need the vibe of a bloody cool environment around me.

I need to mention one more thing.

Did you know, that inside an exceptional agency, there is always a conductor, one who is responsible for this organised chaos? This instrumentalist may not be a hipster, a boozer or even the head honcho. But this person orchestrates. They provide a clear vision of what the agency stands for, what it values, looks like, feels like and acts like. They know the type of people they want; more importantly, they know the type of people they don't want. It's their auditorium and behind the scenes, they pull the strings. If anyone or anything goes against the grain, they lower the curtains and address the 'drain' like a merciless assassin. Make no mistake, these individuals are meticulous planners and are never to be crossed.

And, that my friend, is why some agencies are exceptional.

By the way, did I also mention that exceptional agencies are the most successful agencies? They win the most awards, make the most money and they secure and retain the best talent — both staff and clientele. They produce unrivalled strategic thought and deliver damn hot creative work.

If you question whether culture drives performance, do yourself a favour. Visit a decent agency and think about your wardrobe before you go inside.

Aside

There is a reason for my ramble above.

Yes, I know, it's not always glitter and gold and sometimes the bar fridge in agencies only opens from 1 pm. Nevertheless, I hope you are getting my point. Environments, artefacts, people, processes, principles, guidelines and general persona are what constitute organisational culture. The brilliance of culture is that whoever is leading it can decide on what it looks like. That's right: leaders and founders get to decide. You don't have to be like the crazy agency folk — for some businesses that would be abhorrent and downright wrong. If you want to be the ultra-conservative, professionally polished, risk-averse, process-oriented organisation with intellectual capacity second to none, then go for it. Apart from the hard work and discipline required to make it happen, nothing is stopping you. But please, don't underplay or undervalue its importance.

CORPORATE CULTURE

I would like to step back.

Let's define organisational culture. It has been talked about for 40-plus years and still remains a corporate buzzword. Interestingly, no academics can agree on a single definition, nor align on its key components. Few try to measure it in totality, and for those who do, many question its validity. Fascinating. Whoever cracks this culture nut will make an absolute killing.

Robbie Katanga, in an article from Dr Michael Watkins, nailed the definition for me: 'Culture is how organisations do things'. This works and I need nothing else. When you see consistent and observable behaviours in a workplace, you get an immediate sense of that organisation's culture. Aristotle stated, in essence, that 'we are what we repeatedly do'. You do not obtain cultural understanding from incessant talk, desire or intent. You get it from what gets done.

So why, then, do many of us underplay and underleverage the importance of organisational culture?

A STORY OF FOOLHARDINESS

If you ever spend time working in a beautiful location, be very careful. It distracts your mind and, in my case, makes one partially mad. I was hanging out with my leadership team overlooking Terrigal beach. We were developing our mid-term strategic plan. Terrigal is a beautiful seaside spot on the central coast of New South Wales, Australia.

My team was clever, driven and passionate, and they also had outstanding values. I enjoyed these planning sessions. I strategically positioned myself facing away from the water. I know this sounds strange, but ever since I had a meeting years ago in beautiful Lake Tahoe, Nevada, where I stared out the window and made absolutely no contribution for three entire days, I do my best to avoid spectacular views. As anyone who has worked with me will know, I get easily distracted at the best of times.

Anyway, we were doing our standard vision planning process. When it got to the stage of talking competitive advantage (i.e., what have we got that no-one else has got), the very first thing that was peddled out was 'culture'. I cannot recall who raised it, but the immediacy and uniformity of head nodding in the room was telling. I am not the type to randomly place things on a flipchart, yet I could tell this one would be hard to leave off.

So, being the typical ego-driven leader, I pushed back: 'Come on, people, do we really think we are that different from others? I know we have a good culture, maybe even a great culture, but let's not kid ourselves: everyone else would be saying exactly the same thing. Hand on heart, I can't really say it is unique, different or even defining. Really?'

Aside

Culture will always be a key enabler for strategy, yet you need a good strategy to begin with. I find it fascinating that different leaders use vastly different approaches to strategic planning. Personally, I have always believed in the 'future back approach'. Start with your end point vision in mind, then work back with key milestones that 'have to have happened' to allow you to deliver your future state. I'm not saying this approach is perfect; it just works for me. I like that it removes current realities and limiting beliefs. Impossibility is nothing.

I was first exposed to this way of thinking just outside Boston, Massachusetts, where Reebok Global headquarters were based. An external company called Landmark led the process for us and, even though it was a long time ago now, I recall that it took us two full days to collectively agree on the company's future 'bold statement' position. It was a demanding process. That said, I can still recall it word for word: 'Reebok — Revolutionising the sports and fitness industry through explosive creativity and innovation. One of the fastest growing, most respected and admired brands in the world'. Supported by specific goals and tangible actions, at the time, it was indeed a powerful process.

Funny how little changes over 20-plus years.

Back to Terrigal. For a largely Australian team, it was as though I had just criticised their national cricket legend, Sir Don Bradman. Sacrilege. For the next 20 minutes I was bombarded.

'Why the hell would you not value culture? It's been the cornerstone of our success for 10-plus years. The passion for our segment, the pride for the business, the care for fellow colleagues, the "refusal to lose" mentality. Everyone who joins us or leaves us tells us exactly the same thing — it's vastly different from others and is special and defining. It's a massive strength and we need to nurture, develop and leverage it for all it's worth. You've been on this journey for long enough, what are you thinking Hamish?'

Did I mention they were a passionate bunch?

To this day, I still ask myself why I challenged their position. I think I was just feeling restless.

True, I have always been frustrated with a lack of precision and confidence in measuring cultural dimensions. Yet, as you will read shortly, that is changing. I also know that exceptional cultures are not created overnight. With my insatiable thirst for pace, maybe that was the reason for my challenge? I dismiss this, though, as it would have only fired me up to do it in record speed. Perhaps it was because I've only worked at companies that have had great cultures in the first place? Reebok and Mars in particular were phenomenal. As in this particular case, I like to think I have been part of fostering and growing these cultures, so maybe I simply started taking them for granted?

Above all though, and aside from the distracting beach scenery, I think I was just wrong. I had no excuses.

As a result, I admitted my ignorance and culture was added to the flipchart. To make sure the team did not commit mutiny, I even placed the words in capitals. Since that day, my focus and diligence on all cultural matters has heightened significantly. Thank you, team, for forgiving my moment of madness.

Aside

Encouragingly, measurement within culture is definitely on the move. While we have had satisfaction scores linked to productivity for many a year, most cultural dimensions have been devoid of statistical evidence. Today, there are multiple agencies and methodologies to assist. Once unknown returns for office revamps now have quantifiable ROI data. The same applies in quests for pace, agility and innovation. Lead cultural agencies now have behavioural scientists on staff and it's not uncommon to see econometric statisticians being wheeled out in cultural meetings. A far cry from the smoke and mirrors of yesteryear.

CULTURAL CRISIS

Before outlining some principles of cultural excellence — a.k.a., the practical part — I want to give a sobering reminder of cultural crisis.

Nowadays, it is common practice to read of corporate misconduct. Every day we see examples of financial mismanagement, sexual harassment, quality and safety breaches, remuneration fraud, discriminatory behaviours and competitive breaches to name but a few. It's not unique to regions, countries or industry sectors. But at the crux of the matter is always one thing: culture. If you don't believe me, simply view a parliamentary inquiry finding relating to corporate misconduct. It's always culture.

This is a CEO's worst nightmare. If it happens under your watch, personal values are called into question. Justifiably, in many cases. Exactly for the reasons that cultural assets are so highly valued in an organisation, when they are left in limbo and poorly managed, they can be one of the biggest liabilities imaginable. I recently read an outstanding *Harvard Business Review* article by Sarah Clayton on crisis management. She talked of six indicators that pointed to potential signs of cultural undoing and resulting corporate misconduct. Since reading it, I have committed these to memory:

1. inadequate investment in people

2. lack of accountability

3. lack of diversity, equity and inclusion

4. poor behaviour at the top

5. high-pressure environments

6. unclear ethical standards.

Although this list sounds wide and daunting, the good news is that they are leading indicators. Each is measurable and, with early sight of adverse trends, they can be directly addressed. The key is having the diligence and resolve to keep on top of them. Every leader and director with a conscience or an aversion to jail time should be aware of these.

My final insight relating to culture is a positive one.

When you have a vision of what you and your organisation want to be, culture is your primary gateway to achievement. Being part of an environment that matches your own values and your own ethos is one of the most liberating, enlightening and enjoyable experiences you can have in your career. Find one that aligns with your values and it's a marriage made in heaven.

Alongside safety, culture is unequivocally my number one area of focus.

THE PRACTICAL PART

Cultural awareness

If you ever doubt the importance of culture, or, even worse, forget to stoke it, remind yourself of the simple yet effective principles shown in figure 15.1. Equally, use them as an immediate sense-check as to how culture is led and managed in your organisation.

Figure 15.1: cultural excellence — 10 reminders

If any of these are absent, address them with urgency:

- **Always a strategic lever.** Although many leaders and organisations will declare a cultural focus, test this by looking at their strategic plan. If cultural behaviours are not included, either as a strategic driver or a core enabler, the plan will be suboptimal.

- **Define your cultural vision.** I appreciate this sounds like a given. Unfortunately, for many companies it's not. As a collective leadership team, have you specifically defined what type of culture you desire and need to ensure enduring success? What does this culture look and feel like? Not broad philosophical or grand statements, but specific, prescriptive and easy-to-understand language. The more descriptive, the better. If you are not crystal clear on your cultural vision, it will be impossible for your teams to live up to desired expectations.

  As a leader, this must be one of your lead priorities.

- **Align on cultural dimensions.** What are those specific tangible behaviours that will bring your cultural vision to life? Place a weighting of importance against each of them. Where are you today and where do you want to get to? If there are dimensions of innovation, creativity, agility or pace, have you established the metrics and acceptable levels of tolerance for success?

- **Commit with time and resources.** If culture is part of your strategic plan, it needs to receive dedicated and allocated strategic resources. Do not fall into the trap of thinking culture will happen on its own. Allocate passionate and competent people against specific cultural dimensions and support them with adequate resources, recognition and reward.

- **Communicate with clarity.** The way you describe the organisation's culture is paramount. Employees and potential new starters need to have clarity on the culture that is desired and expected. When done well it provides boundaries for people to follow and ensures that they act in a way that mirrors company values.

  Make sure that you portray this clarity within all recruitment processes as well. It's an outstanding way to market your business for ongoing talent attraction.

- **Execute with mercenary discipline.** My only advice on this area is not to downplay cultural accountability. Many will treat cultural progress as desirable, not essential, but it can be a costly error. Hold people to account exactly the way you would with a growth, efficiency or earnings target.

- **Measure — including early alarm bells.** Ensure that measurement metrics focus on leading indicators. These early alarm bells can be invaluable. Most organisations will have an effective Sales & Operations (S&OP) or Integrated Business Planning (IBP) process. Cultural measurement should be a key part of this. It will ensure management accountability and senior leadership visibility.

- **Stoke, fuel and adapt.** Although I love transformation, the majority of cultural work should be evolutionary, with continuous improvement. The exception being where you have a major declared breakdown (think of the 2019 financial and banking royal commissions). Critically, do not start cultural work and let it fade. As with any capability, it needs constant fuel.

- **No exceptions, no weaknesses.** This can be challenging: it is the true test of a leader's resolve and commitment to culture. When you allow cultural abuse to occur — particularly at senior levels — it sends two clear messages. Firstly, that culture is only 'a nice to do' within the company. And secondly, that leadership commitment is negligible or flawed at best. Both are unacceptable perceptions to deliver.

- **Never take for granted, never.** Even if you are in a beautiful beachside location.

MODELS FOR THE WHITEBOARD

Change and Cultural Impact model

I have always liked the clarity and simplicity of this model (see figure 15.2).

Unfortunately, it's forgotten by many.

In my experience, organisational design (OD) or structural change is one of the very first things that average managers and average leaders do. In the majority of cases, it is distracting and the final impact is vastly overstated. I also believe it's perceived as the easy option to take and seldom leads to the root cause of the issue or opportunity in question. (Yes, there are exceptions.)

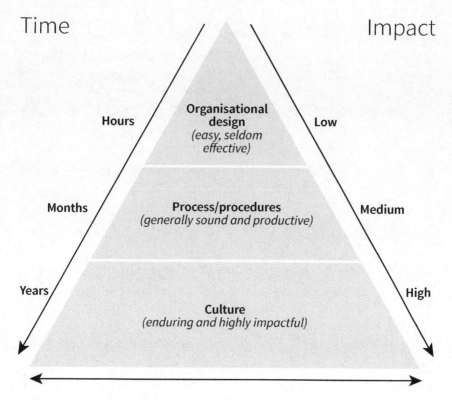

Figure 15.2: change management impact cycle

Process and procedural elements take a little longer to embed, yet their impact on continuous improvement is generally sound.

Cultural change, however, always has high impact, and when done effectively, is enduring. It will not happen overnight. Exceptional leaders realise this and will have infinite patience to ensure success.

THE CRITIQUE

A brief review from cultural experts Nick Tucker and Ben Bars, CEO and co-founder of We Are Unity, Sydney, Australia.

In corporate circles, 'culture' is a buzzword that executives understand intellectually — but more often than not, can't translate into tangible, meaningful action. Just like human emotions, there are no hard and fast rules for culture: it's not black and white, but an interpretation of continually changing circumstances that come in multiple shades of grey.

Like emotions, you can usually tell when culture is inauthentic. And even though we can't see it, the impact of culture is always unmissable: When the 2019 Australian Royal Commission demanded the Big Four banks cough up an initial bill for $2.4 billion in regulatory costs, the root cause identified was… culture. When AMP saw their share price halved in response to allegations of board misconduct, the root cause identified was… culture. When the FMCG industry is forced to buy its innovation rather than create it themselves, the root cause identified is… culture. And outside the boardroom, when Australian cricketers were caught cheating in South Africa during the infamous 'ball tampering scandal', the root cause identified was… you got it.

Regardless of intent, many leaders struggle to understand, design and drive the right culture. Their struggle is indeed real:

- **The myth of the silver bullet.** A preponderance of leaders — 76 per cent — report that their organisational culture needs to change significantly over the next three to five years. However even if this improves, there will still never be such a thing as one 'perfect' culture. All models that propose this neglect to laser in on the context of an organisation's unique business strategy, and the priorities needed for that equally unique culture journey.

- **The absence of strategy.** Every successful culture design needs to start with an honest and realistic view of the right culture to deliver a unique business strategy. Yet 43 per cent of executives report a misalignment between culture and strategy. To consciously design a culture that delivers, start by identifying the mindsets and behaviours that will unlock your strategy. If innovation is your goal, your culture design should allow for deliberate self-disruption and support psychological safety, so that your people feel free to challenge and embrace a 'test and learn' mentality.

- **The absence of proof.** With only 12 per cent of organisations using predictive analytics to support decision making, the fact is that most organisations can't prove the link between culture and commercial outcomes. And while the traditional belief has always been that designing a culture of engagement drives performance, organisations now need to prove the impact of culture on financial performance to get buy-in from the board — and any other powers that be.

So, forget the title of this chapter. This is how you make culture matter:

- Consciously design it based on your business strategy.

- Stop chasing engagement scores and instead hold each member of the executive team accountable for driving the right culture.

- Prove the impact on financial performance by measuring the right things.

PS — at We Are Unity our definition is 'Commercial culture refers to employee mindsets and behaviours that contribute to achieving an organisation's strategy'.

Chapter 16

Constant Dissatisfaction

Considered to be the godfather of American psychology, William James was a man after my own heart.

He held some pretty firm views on the topic of satisfaction. According to him, the struggle to alleviate dissatisfaction and return to a satisfied state is what drives human activity and human development.

Big call.

But it's a call that supports me being a miserable bugger who is always wanting more.

I think we would have got on well.

THE MESSAGE ·······················

In this chapter I'll get a bit into the theory of dissatisfaction and why I feel it works for me (and the pitfalls of this approach for others), but then I want to stop talking directly about dissatisfaction. Although I like the subject and, to me, it's a cool discussion point, the real message behind this chapter is slightly different.

The message goes like this: it does not matter whether you have a driving thirst for change or you are completely comfortable with the status quo. What matters is that you're aware of your preference, and that you're aware of your talents relating to that preference. As a result, you need to get yourself an assignment or a job that's right for you, your company and that particular point in time. This is what matters.

···

For as long as I can remember I have been told two things: the first is that I am constantly dissatisfied. The second is that I was born with a constant frown on my face.

I am okay with the first comment; I get it completely. In regard to the second, I begrudgingly accept it, although it pains me to do so. (My old man went pretty bald, and a receding hairline coupled with a frown-marked forehead is never a good combination.)

The way it has been explained to me over the years is as follows: there are two types of dissatisfaction. One is labelled healthy dissatisfaction. If you haven't cottoned on already, this is the good type of dissatisfaction. I don't have this one. Healthy dissatisfaction can be described as beneficially looking into areas of needed improvement and having a healthy level of desire for relevant and adequate change.

The other type of dissatisfaction is constant dissatisfaction. This is what I have. It can be described as never being satisfied with the status quo, even if that status quo is working. It also means constantly, consistently and relentlessly striving for improvement and advancement. At times, striving behaviour can turn into demanding behaviour.

Personally, I don't think my constant dissatisfaction is as bad as the characterisation I just gave. That said, I did notice my head nodding in agreement as I typed its definition. I don't know how I got into this camp of constant dissatisfaction, but to date it's worked for me and has had no major adverse effects. (I'll get to its impact on others shortly. Interestingly, I highly value consistency and stability in family and friendships; I think it's this balance that makes me strive for continual improvement and change within a work setting.)

Back to a broader question. Why do we need dissatisfaction?

According to American psychologist William James, 'it is the experience of dissatisfaction that moves society ever onwards'. Numerous psychological journals support this belief, but I prefer to talk of dissatisfaction in much simpler terms.

I describe it as 'an itch that just needs to be scratched', a compulsion that is almost impossible to leave untouched or unsolved and cannot be left alone. I believe that at one time or another, all of us have had this feeling.

Conversely, what happens when you feel a true level of satisfaction?

You do nothing. That's right, you do absolutely nothing—and why should you? When you're in a state of deep satisfaction, you don't have the energy or the need to do anything. This is not laziness, inertia or even apathy; it's simply total contentment. It's a very cool feeling to have total contentment and, unfortunately for restless people like myself, it does not happen too often.

The one thing that we universally know about contentment is that it does not drive you towards action. Discontent and dissatisfaction do, however, and this is why I like them.

Aside

'Don't confuse motion for impact.'

When I saw this slogan in Facebook's London office, it instantly appealed to me. We consistently see this very flaw in ourselves and, on occasions, within others. Countless hours of well-intended activity resulting in nonexistent or negligible results.

I love simple phrases like this. They're basic reminders when you're in the midst of the daily grind that make you stop, reflect and ask questions: 'Am I making a tangible difference?' If the answer is no, change is required. As a leader, I also ask the same question of my teams and the total business. Sometimes it will require an attitudinal change and at other times it will compel a behavioural shift. Either way, it inspires a commitment to do things differently.

I have also become very curious about a concept called 'the relativity of time'. It is not linked to Einstein. Rather, from listening to a podcast by Joe Rogan! One guest interview focused on the limited amount of time we have prior to impending death. A potentially morbid topic, yet it turned out to be incredibly motivational.

Without going into too much detail, this individual inspirationally began packing as much 'value-add stuff' as humanly possible into his life. It started with quality time with his ageing parents before leading onto an almost compulsive state of accelerated learning. Every week for one entire year, he attempted to become the very best he could possibly be within a nominated subject of interest. One week he would hire a grandmaster chess champion to train him in the art of chess. The next week, a leading Everest Sherpa to coach him on technical altitude mountaineering. The next, a national philharmonic orchestra member to tutor the double bass. The list went on. This was clearly a very driven and impressive, not to mention wealthy, individual. It also sounded bloody exhausting.

Either way, I relay this story because it relates back to that Facebook slogan. If we genuinely believe that time is limited — which I think most of us post 30 years of age do — then surely impact versus motion is mission critical. Life is way too short otherwise.

CHANNELING DISSATISFACTION

One of my most recent bosses is one who I probably admire and revere the most. In fact, it took me a good six months to stop feeling intimidated around her. Not because she was a tyrant or overly demanding — far from it. It was simply because she was so good at everything that she did.

There is a great skill set that I am envious of. It is the ability to be at your optimal best every single day. From a mindfulness perspective, they label this as being in a constant 'state of Beta'. Beta brainwaves are associated with a heightened state of alertness, logic and critical reasoning. This allows you to be at your very best. Like most people, I strive for everyday Beta, yet at times I have failed miserably with definitely my share of off days. My boss in question appeared to have bugger all of these off days!

Anyway, the reason for telling you this, is that she gave me one of the best pieces of advice. In addition, she also gave me one of the worst — she may tell you differently. Both relate to my persona of constant dissatisfaction.

Let me start with the best. A few years back, I had the great privilege of taking a two-month sabbatical as part of my long service leave. Apart from it being a wonderful opportunity for self-indulgence (which it was, by the way), it also sent an incredible message to the wider associate base. Here was a company and a senior leader who role-modelled the importance of balance. It showcased to others what was clearly acceptable, possible and indeed encouraged by the organisation. The number of people, locally and globally, who thanked me for this was astounding. In turn, I was very thankful to the company for allowing it to happen.

Anyway, back to the advice. Just prior to my return to the business, Fiona called me for a general check-in. She said, 'Hamish, I want you to treat your return to the office as though it is your first day of being with the company. Fresh eyes, a totally new perspective, a blank sheet of paper, no pre-set rules and a renewed drive and vigour for success'.

I don't know about you, but for me there are some people who say things in a way that just hits your motivational button. This resonated with my style, my desire and my natural state of constant dissatisfaction. Interestingly, it ended up being one of the most successful years the business had. Thank you, Fiona. Small things make exceptional leaders. This was one of them.

Now, here comes the bad advice.

Years earlier, when we had left Europe and headed back to Australia (for the second time), the business was incredibly supportive and found me a role heading up the Regional Food business. It was an opportunity to join a very successful business with some great brands, exceptional people and an outstanding track record of growth. Additionally, I was now part of a global leadership team which was a great developmental stretch.

Apart from the typical mentoring from all concerned, including the standard line from the family owners, 'Don't screw it up, Hamish', my new boss, Fiona, pulled me aside: 'Look, I know your last few roles have been turnaround situations. Those businesses needed change and you needed to come in and create a burning platform to do so. But in this case, the business has been doing well so I suggest for the first three-plus months you just sit back, reflect, observe and really educate yourself before inserting your standard change agenda'. I'm sure she articulated this better than above, but you get the picture.

Now, let me be clear. This is not bad advice per se, and for most people this would have worked perfectly well. For me, though, it didn't.

Although the business continued to perform admirably during those initial three to six months, it and I could have done better. Been more proactive, more productive and stretched further. I was not at my best and, as a result, I do not think the business performed to the potential it should have. Luckily, there were exceptional people in place to ensure that it continued doing well.

In practice, when I operate in a constant state of dissatisfaction, I:

- try to look for things before they are broken
- challenge current paradigms to see if they're optimal
- ask questions of processes to see if they are as efficient and effective as they could be
- set stretch targets to force new ways of thinking and new approaches to challenges and opportunities
- never stay satisfied with current levels of performance.

I attempt to do these things very early within my tenure and within any new position that I have taken.

This is when I'm at my best and, in all cases to date, when I have been my most successful. Taking a back seat, reflecting and accepting current practices as effective simply doesn't work for me. I'm not the bull in the china shop that causes chaos, but I am the one who strives for and instigates continuous change and improvement. I should have followed this approach and style from day one upon returning to Australia.

Aside

Although I say this was not ideal advice from my boss, the real reflection point was a personal one. This was my third regional president assignment. Although you are always learning at all stages of your career, I was not a fresh-faced executive. By this stage of my tenure, I knew myself better than ever. I knew my strengths as well as my development areas. Critically, I also knew which style and approach made me and others perform at our collective best. I should have followed this from day one. My responsibility, and lesson learned. That said, using my boss as a bit of a scapegoat makes for a better chapter.

A DISSATISFIED PERSON'S APPROACH TO BUSINESS MODELS

One of the better management books I have read (and actually finished) is *The First 90 Days* by Dr Michael Watkins. He talks about a simple quadrant model that describes four stages of business maturity:

1. Start-up

2. Turnaround

3. Realignment

4. Sustaining success.

In his recent work, Michael also introduces a fifth stage called Accelerated Growth (part of his STARS framework) but I will leave you to discover more on this yourself. Each quadrant requires a specific competency set and a different leadership approach. I like this because it reflects the importance of getting the right person to do the right job at the right time. We term this 'the right fit'.

I'll detail his original model at the end of this chapter, but in the meantime let me give two examples of how someone who is constantly dissatisfied views these initial quadrants.

'SUSTAINING SUCCESS'? IMPOSSIBLE

Example one: I actually struggle with having a quadrant even labelled 'sustaining success'.

I definitely understand the position in the model and why the author has included it. My apprehension is that when we use the term 'sustain' — or similar words such as maintain, conserve, uphold, protect or safeguard — it leads to one thing. Decline.

In my experience, when people and teams hear the word 'sustain', tension valves are instantly released. While they are under no illusion as to how difficult a maintain position will be to achieve, inherently, pressure levels decline. I'm not questioning the goal itself — there will always be times when a flat or declining target is necessary — but I am questioning the behaviours that result from it.

Individuals and teams are often given sustain targets with little motivational context behind them. This happens at regional, market, portfolio and even departmental levels. It also happens frequently.

Take these two communication scenarios. (The word 'brand' could easily be substituted by 'region', 'market' or 'unit'.)

- Team A: Market analysis shows there is limited growth potential within your part of the brand portfolio. It has had declining levels of penetration and flat category levels for the past three years. It is clearly a headwind category and as a result, we have set you a flat sales and profit target for the year.

- Team B: Every brand within our portfolio has a crucial part to play. Your brand needs to be successful in order to fuel and fund the investment of our tailwind growth categories of x and y. If you guys fail, it will be impossible for the rest of the portfolio to grow and as a result, we will not succeed as a business. We need you to achieve a flat sales and profit target versus last year. We know this will be a big challenge. It is an extremely tough category and competitor set that you play within. However, this is a no negotiation and no debate target. The business needs you to achieve this goal and it remains mission critical for you to do so. You will have our full support and focus to make this a reality.

While the language of these examples may appear exaggerated, they are not. This happens regularly within virtually every organisation, across every facet of the business. There is always a perception that one party is loved and recognised more than another. If you don't believe me, take a step back and reflect on how it works within your business:

- Is one department talked about more than another?

- Do growth channels get recognised more than those in decline?

- Is an emerging region showcased more than a developed one?

- Do new tailwind categories get loved, revered and rewarded ahead of headwind segments?

- Do certain individuals get more leadership time and agenda space than others?

The list goes on.

Now, I'm not saying this is fair. Regardless as to whether we like it or not, there are only so many places where we can focus our energies. The key to successful leadership, however, is ensuring that where you do have visible presence, you make it effective and you make it motivational. In the example given, I think there would be considerable differences in passion and drive between individuals who sit in Team A versus Team B, purely because of communication.

Motivational communication and relevant context are needed across all levels of an organisation. In particular, never let a 'sustaining success' position go unchecked on the pressure gauge.

REALIGNMENT: TRICKIER THAN IT LOOKS

Example two: Having constant dissatisfaction also makes me look at the 'realignment' quadrant with a slightly different lens from others.

To me, 'realignment' essentially means that we are doing well, but we need slight amendments here and there to keep being successful. I have always felt that a 'turnaround' situation is easier than that of realignment.

When one is in a turnaround situation, the team is already in a world of pain. People want answers and, importantly, direction. A leader can come in, declare a very obvious position of a burning platform, set a clear strategic path forward and, even if that chosen plan is not the perfect one, as long as it's communicated with conviction, people will follow. They desperately want someone to lead and take charge, and by heck if that leader is passionate and compelling enough, they will fully support them. And why not? Everything else they have tried has failed dismally. The worst thing possible within a business that requires turnaround is confusion and a lack of clarity on the path forward. People don't want endless discussion; they want firm and immediate direction.

In my mind, a realignment situation is slightly more complex. It requires a different and I believe a heightened level of leadership tact to ensure success. It involves getting the business to appreciate that, while they have been successful in the past, change will be needed if they want to be successful going forward. It's trying to ignite a behavioural change when people don't see the need to change.

Although difficult, this is an awesome leadership challenge. It requires you to honour the past but equally compel people to believe that they need to do something different, and do so quickly. I have had numerous challenging experiences on this, and each has been super valuable from a learning perspective.

Aside

Even as I write this, my main takeaway from all the quadrants (excluding the start-up quadrant), is that you should have a mindset of treating every business as though it's in a turnaround situation. No surprise that a person who is constantly dissatisfied should think this.

DISSATISFACTION'S FALLOUT

Okay. Prior to the practical part, I want you to understand the adverse impact my style of constant dissatisfaction can have on others.

When you are constantly looking ahead and wanting 'next', there can be unintended consequences of low recognition. Current or previous levels of effort and achievement are quickly overlooked or bypassed. With awareness and constant self-reminders, I have learned to address this. As a leader of others, it's vital I do so.

Next is what's discussed in chapter 14, The hardest part of a decision. I need to allow reflectors adequate time for true insight and learning. A constant state of dissatisfaction does not always permit this to happen.

Additionally, too much change can lead to distraction and instability for individuals, teams and organisations. Particularly if it lowers focus on core revenue and profit segments. Change levels must be closely monitored, with clear attention and support given to change management capabilities — talent, processes and procedures.

Despite these negative impacts, the best way I manage constant dissatisfaction is by surrounding myself with exceptional talent and listening to them, big time. It's essential that I have a leadership team who think differently from me, have a risk profile that is diverse from my own, and, importantly, can openly and consistently challenge me. Fortunately, I have always had this.

A word of advice

I once expressed my frustration to a business coach at constantly having to slow down and wait for others to catch up in a work sense. I expressed that others didn't have the same desire for change as I did, that they were reluctant to take risks and were nervous of potentially adverse outcomes.

Yep, pretty juvenile complaints. I was put back in my box very quickly:

> Stop your moaning, Hamish, and take control of the situation. Do the following: Never slow down, as this is what gives personal energy and drive. To enable this, you need to delegate more than ever. Not standard delegation, but delegation with total freedom and autonomy. Set your stretch goals and let them achieve them exactly the way they want to. You can support and coach, but don't ever contemplate directing them to do it your way. Finally, accept mistakes and imperfections. Greater than you have ever done before. Unless you do this, no-one will ever take on your change agenda as they will get hurt by doing so.

Tough, sage and invaluable advice.

A former Reebok boss and great mate of mine in the UK told me that the art of effective delegation was for every task delegated to you, give two back! Thanks, Steve. I love this and I think my coach mentioned above may have heard the same story.

THE PRACTICAL PART

Making the most of constant dissatisfaction

Many of the headlines in figure 16.1 are covered throughout this book. For those that I have not discussed, I bring these concepts alive with further clarification and examples on my website. The purpose of including these is to provide specific concepts and frameworks that will allow a mindset of dissatisfaction to work effectively. Not one that is random or scattered in approach; one with considered discipline that will allow efficient and successful implementation. If curious, feel free to explore.

Fringe to the core *(lifeboat vs oil tanker)*	**Lead change** *(don't just manage it)*	**The 30% Rule**
Use the portfolio *(risk and boldness)*	**Outside–in perspective**	**Ahead of the change curve, always**
Start-up mindset *(think like a founder)*	**Problems are better than opportunities**	**Roles for everyone**
Enjoy the journey *(not the destination)*	**Love red** *(red vs green scorecard)*	**Language of entrepreneurs**
Believing and knowing *(never the same thing)*	**Open challenge and open opinions**	**Impact** *(not motion)*
Agility *(big A vs little A)*	**Repeat — but bigger, better, faster**	**No regrets**
Performance vs general measures	**Success vs mastery**	**Q = A + 1**
Extremities of options	**Turnaround mentality**	**Maintain means decline**

Figure 16.1: constant dissatisfaction — organised chaos that works

MODELS FOR THE WHITEBOARD

Stages of Business Maturity

As mentioned, figure 16.2 is a great model from Dr Michael Watkins (*The First 90 Days*). I reference this framework whenever I talk about a particular skill set and capability that is required within the business. It's equally applicable to an organisation, market, segment, unit or function. I suggest you throw it on the whiteboard and discuss what quadrant position is relevant for you today. Value-add discussion will focus on specific competencies, behaviours, rules and talent required for each quadrant. Remember, however, regardless of what quadrant you are in, I urge you to start with a mindset of dissatisfaction and constantly search for improvement rather than maintaining status quo.

Right fit
(right job, right person, right time)

Turnround	Realignment
	My favourite leadership challenge — convincing others they are not quite as good as they think they are.

The First 90 Days

Start-up	Sustaining success
	Motivational and inspirational messaging is critical. In its absence, inevitable decline.

Figure 16.2: stages of business maturity

THE CRITIQUE

A brief rebuttal from one of the leading global customer-centric thinkers, Oli Morton, Chief Customer and Operations Officer, Kellogg's, Chicago, USA.

· ·

Although I firmly sit on the 'constant dissatisfaction' side, the key to success is knowing your own preference, understanding how it will work in the situations you face and being able to leverage it.

Your ability to do this will either create energy for yourself and those around you, or drain it. So, not much at stake, then!

To build preference awareness, I contend that you 'need to do'. Embrace as many contrasting situations and experiences as possible — from startup to turnaround — and do so early in your career. Treat it like an experiment, as there is no better way than trial and error. You will soon work out what gets you leaping out of bed to attack the day.

Next is working out how you harness your own energy and amplify it to those around you. What does it take to get to our destination without slowing down?

I have found the answer is always the same: if you are clear on your purpose, you can create an environment of stretch, energy and freedom to deliver.

Because that's what the great leaders do.

They know who they are, they understand what motivates them and those around them, and they can shape and create a purpose that captures the hearts and minds of their people.

In *The Last Dance* — the story of the Chicago Bulls basketball team in the 1990s — the pivotal moment for the Bulls is when coach Phil Jackson (who has the nickname 'the Zen Master') enables Michael Jordan to channel his constant dissatisfaction from making himself the best in the world, to making the *team* the best in the world. The real beauty isn't what Michael Jordan became, but rather his energy, relentlessness and standards that enabled the team to become the best version of themselves. As we know, collectively, they performed well ahead of their skill set.

It's a great example of how a leader and team understood their preference, leveraged their drive and achieved their purpose. This is satisfaction.

Chapter 17
The Authentic You

Much has been written about authenticity. Too much, in fact.

Theories and quotes, books and speeches.

Everyone has a view and each will claim authority. I hope mine has perspective, validity and brevity.

Oscar Wilde's perfect take on this issue: 'Be yourself, everyone else is taken'.

Crystal clear.

Oh to be Oscar Wilde; it would save a lot of time and trees.

THE MESSAGE ·······················

This is going to be a reasonably short chapter. At my last count, there were 237 books pertaining to authenticity and I don't want to add to deforestation on this subject.

My overarching message: it is way too exhausting to lead two lives. Be 100 per cent authentic and lead one life. You will be astonished at how liberating and beneficial it is.

···

I like this definition of authenticity: 'Being authentic means being true to yourself through perfectly aligned thoughts, words and actions'. What you think and say in life are matched by your behaviours.

I value authenticity for three main reasons.

The first is that I want to be the best possible version of myself, and I can only do this when I am being me. I'm at my happiest when I'm at ease with who I am and the way I am. Not in exhausting 'prove' mode, not trying to overly impress and not imitating the actions or behaviours of someone I am not. It has taken me a long time to appreciate this.

Secondly, I want to experience relationships with depth and unquestionable quality. You know by now how much I value relationships. When I'm honest, transparent and vulnerable, my connections go to new levels. When I'm not, they're superficial at best.

Finally, I want to be the best leader I can be. Research has shown that authentic employees have higher satisfaction and engagement levels. They are happier at work, possess a stronger sense of community, are more inspirational and have lower levels of stress. But unless I portray authentic leadership, few will follow this path.

Not being my authentic self has also led to difficulties.

TWO HAMISHES, TWO RESULTS

A prime example was venturing into my first managing director assignment. My predecessor told me that I needed to change my approach when dealing with global colleagues. My use of relaxed humour and personal storytelling was apparently fine for my direct teams, yet senior international folk would expect and need a different Hamish. More professional and more serious. The message was 'don't even contemplate showing your real side'.

As a result, two Hamishes ensued. My natural self worked effectively for both me and the region that I was leading. But the other Hamish was disingenuous. He surfaced when I was around senior global folk. He was not ineffective, but he was not me. He was reserved, distant and certainly did not enter the depth of relationships that I had developed with my local teams.

I seldom enjoyed those initial global interactions. I did not benefit from the amazing diversity of talent that surrounded me. That still pains me. Interestingly, the day I started being my authentic self, global team meetings and interactions became enjoyable and unbelievably inspiring. I don't blame my predecessor for this feedback. I blame myself for being slow to realise that it was simply the wrong advice for me.

Not being authentic also made me tired. I found it exhausting maintaining the two Hamishes. Acting, appearing and behaving differently is draining, arduous and above all, fatiguing. I found it challenging to improve and focus on myself, let alone my imposter shadow.

Being inauthentic also made me uncomfortable. There is something very unsettling when you are not portraying your true self. It is not deceitful, yet it is deceiving. I never liked this feeling.

Aside

Whenever you receive feedback, I suggest you let 98 per cent of it go through to the keeper. Listen with true intent, yet only take on board those one or two areas that truly resonate with you. If not, it has the potential to drive you crazy. Listen, refine, but don't fundamentally change the authentic you: try not to forget this.

MY WAKE-UP CALL

Things got real when I was in my early thirties. I had the opportunity to go to Colorado Springs. About 100 kilometres south of Denver and at the eastern edge of the Rocky Mountains, it is a mecca for outdoor lovers. Despite the odd headache — it's more than 1800 metres above sea level — the air is unbelievably clean, and you cannot help but feel a true sense of escapism.

I was there for a five-day leadership course run by a company called CCL (Center for Creative Leadership). They remain one of the pre-eminent leadership institutes, with an array of outstanding coaches and cutting-edge practices. Leadership courses of this nature are fairly commonplace today, but back then it was unique and I was lucky to be one of the early Mars cohort to experience it.

If I could sum up what that week was about, it was essentially five full days purely about me. Nothing specific to the business, just learning about who I am as a person. What makes me tick, and how I can become better. It was self-indulgent, and I loved it! Along the way, I completed more forms and assessments than I thought humanly possible. I got daily feedback from coaches and peers, conducted personal health assessments, did morning hikes and runs, and, as per any good leadership course, ate a shed load of expensive organic kale. (In case you haven't gathered by now, I dislike kale.)

On day three, in my standard one-on-one morning coaching session, my coach, a US consultant named Carol, was more blunt than usual: 'Hamish, let's get down to it. My concern is not one of opportunity or ability. My concern is that I have no idea what you want out of this process. We can play around the edges or we can go deeper. What do you really want from all this?'

Although I am open to new stuff and new insights, when they're personal, I struggle. After going around in circles, she finally got it out of me. I admitted, 'I'm not really enjoying my role. I don't mind the work that I do. I find it interesting and I like most of the people, but I just don't know if this corporate and leadership stuff is really me.'

As I mentioned in chapter 3, The man who used to smile, a few years earlier when living in the Netherlands, I had discovered that I needed to chill out more and not take life too seriously. To be fair, I had changed, and I was doing okay on that front. But this was bigger. I was questioning if this whole corporate game was right for me.

My dilemma was made worse because so many parts of leadership appealed to me. My competitive nature was constantly fuelled. Intellectually, I was challenged daily. I enjoyed inspiring, developing and growing others. Even when I had to be the 'bad cop' and make difficult decisions, I knew that I could make them and convey them in a manner that was more respectful and more caring than others around me. Additionally, I loved the vast array of perspective and diversity of thought that was afforded me within these roles.

So, why the lack of enjoyment, and why did it just not feel right for me?

A good coach doesn't muck around, and Carol was a good coach. Almost instantaneously, she replied: 'Stop trying to be the executive you think others want you to be and be the leader you want to be.' Not quite as succinct as Oscar Wilde, but not far off.

Over the final two days of the course, we dug deep. We identified the specific qualities and attributes that I wanted to possess and portray as a leader. These were the traits that resonated with me, that were fully aligned with my personality and value set. We also discussed those actions and behaviours that didn't sit well with me: those characteristics I had witnessed through others or perceived as being important to others but not me. This helped form my personal leadership brand, discussed in chapter 6, Noticed, Remembered, Understood.

I truly believe that week in Colorado was responsible for me continuing my leadership journey. Carol, greatly appreciated.

Aside

When I was in my twenties and living in England, I used to travel back home to New Zealand once every year or so. On one occasion, I stopped over in Sydney to visit friends and managed to secure a meeting with leading executive search firm Egon Zehnder. From my side, I viewed it as a pretty casual meet and greet opportunity. It was likely that in three to four years' time, I would be returning to Australasia and I simply wanted to get myself on the radar of a few key folk. Nothing more. Anyway, I thought I had a great session with Jane, their lead principal, and was feeling rather pleased with myself as we stood to say goodbye.

Just before reaching the door, she nonchalantly said, 'Very nice to meet you Hamish, but do know that I will not be placing you'. I stopped dead in my tracks. Apart from the fact that I wasn't actually looking for a job, what was she thinking? I thought I had been on pretty good form.

'I will not be placing you as throughout this entire session, you have simply put on a façade and haven't exposed anything to me. The leaders I deal with are only those who are transparent and authentic. Enjoy your day, Hamish.' Wow, she was good!

Cut to three years later. I was now based in the Netherlands and we were seriously considering a move to Australia within the next 18 months. On another holiday back home, I again stopped in Sydney and managed to secure another meeting with Jane. This time, I was prepared. I nailed it. I didn't break down in tears, yet I wasn't far off. I was more open, transparent and vulnerable than ever before. Martin Scorsese would have marvelled at my performance. Standing up to leave, I knew I had done well. Her parting words: 'Great to see you again, Hamish. Oh, by the way, I still won't be placing you'. Bloody hell, she wasn't good, she was exceptional! I was still in theatre mode, acting my way through the interview, instead of revealing the real me. She'd delivered a massive lesson to a very naive and cocky young executive.

Needless to say, I did finally end up getting the message and today, authentic leadership is definitely one of my core strengths. Thank you, Jane, as hard lessons like this one bring it home.

THE PRACTICAL PART

Being the 'authentic you'

As mentioned, there are thousands of texts and models relating to authenticity. I am not going to add to this list. The one author I want to highlight is Professor Bill George, from the Harvard Business School. Figure 17.1 is his Authentic Leadership Model. Simple, relatable and effective — well worth a look.

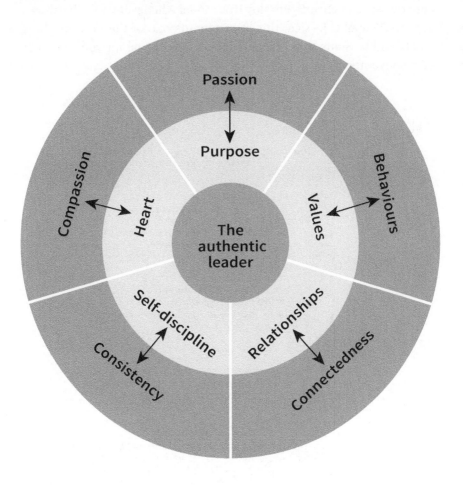

Figure 17.1: Authentic Leadership Model

MODELS FOR THE WHITEBOARD

The Imposter Syndrome

I reference the imposter syndrome on many occasions throughout this book. It's a psychological pattern in which one doubts one's accomplishments and has a persistent fear of being exposed as a fraud. Figure 17.2 arose from a personal coaching session that I once had while walking along a beach in Freshwater, Sydney. A beautiful setting but a tough message to absorb. Employ this model whenever you're battling a bout of self doubt. Jessica, this still remains one of the best coaching models and sessions that I have received. Thank you for your patience and perseverance!

Types

Dismissive
Dismissing your accomplishments, downplaying your efforts/abilities/experience

Inadequate
Regardless of how well you perform, including praise from others, you think you could and should have done better.

Fraudulent
You feel like a fraudster who will be found out. You are faking the role and genuinely not fulfilling it.

Inauthentic
Adapting yourself to get those in authority to like you — using charm and sensitivity to win others over (intellectual inauthenticity).

Unforgiving
Unforgiving of mistakes. Anything less than perfection equals failure. Rather than learning from your shortcomings you give yourself a really hard time about them.

Figure 17.2: the dreaded imposter syndrome

Solutions

Adjust expectations
Practise the 80 per cent rule. Bypass your usual perfectionistic self standards and commit to completing things to 80 per cent perfect and see if anyone notices the difference.

Understand the P/N ratio
For every negative aspect of your performance that you identify, list three to five things that you did well. Adopt this philosophy with feedback from others as well — listen to their praise and take it in. Research supports this theory.

Practise authenticity
Learn to let go of the phoniness or intellectual inauthenticity. Including towards those you desire to impress.

Figure 17.2: the dreaded imposter syndrome (*cont'd*)

THE CRITIQUE

A brief review from Juan Bautista Martin Alonso, President of KIND International, New York, USA.

. . . .

In this chapter, Hamish speaks of one of the single most relevant contributors to a happy, fulfilling life. I would like to remind us that we only live one life, that it is futile and short, and that one day you must look back and feel proud and happy about what you achieved and the legacy you left behind. It is simply impossible to do that without having shown the authentic you!

This is what the chapter is about.

As Hamish expresses eloquently, authenticity is about speaking from your heart; it is about focusing more on how you communicate and why you behave the way you do, rather than what you say. In order to live a consistent life, it is critically important to dig deep about who you are and what are the values that drive you: then, being authentic becomes much easier, since it is about ensuring that all our acts will be in line with that short list of core values that make you the person you are.

When we think of leadership in the corporate world, we tend to put the focus and energy around the 'bright' side of leadership, making a successful leader as close to perfection as possible. What we tend to underestimate is that behind that image, there is a human with his or her strengths and weaknesses, a person who struggles, as any other, to have a happy and meaningful life. And authentic leadership is precisely what makes them the successful leader they are.

One person said to me one day that the shortest distance between two points is truth. With truth, you can avoid superficial interactions, you can build a relationship out of positive intent and make the impact on others that you would like to make.

Remember that success in life is not about behaving as expected in the world, but building a lasting legacy that will make life worth it to be lived to the full! The closer you can live according to your values and lead from them, the higher the chances of achieving a successful life.

Good luck with it.

Chapter 18

Who Is Writing Your Agenda?

Some people just have the 'It' factor.

I guess it helps when that someone looks like this bloke.

Mario Gabriele Andretti is an Italian-born American former racing car driver. He has the heritage, the name, the sunglasses, the cars and always the leather jacket. He is one of only two drivers to have won races in Formula 1, IndyCar, World Sportscar Champs and NASCAR.

As somewhat of a wannabe petrol-head myself, I like him a lot.

The other reason I like him is for his quote, 'If you are in control, you are not driving fast enough'. It's my all-time favourite and my number one go to when describing my ideal state of mind.

The key is having a go in the first place. It starts with setting your own agenda. Not executing another's, but leading and creating your own.

And who knows, just maybe we can secure an ounce of that 'It' factor along the way.

THE MESSAGE ·

People follow leaders; they work for managers.

This is why I have chosen to lead. It motivates and inspires me. I like to set my own agenda wherever I can. This means doing it in a manner where I set the pace. Not leaving it to chance and not leaving it in the hands of others, regardless of how capable or well-intentioned they may be.

I prefer an approach that enhances my odds of winning. Although I haven't always done so, I now religiously try to plan my own journey. No reason why you cannot as well.

· ·

Let me start with a reality check that happened to me back in 2005.

It was during my pet-care days at Albury–Wodonga. As Marketing Director, I had what I would term an extended honeymoon period within the business. For four-plus years we had some amazing success as an organisation. I was surrounded by exceptional people and exceptional brands. It was easy to impress. My natural path was into general management and the company had generously sent me on various leadership courses and MBA-equivalent development programs. By fortune or good planning, I had also been consistently rated as one of the leading global Mars associates. I apologise if this sounds arrogant; it's not intended to be. I'm hoping to illustrate that, regardless of your results or how well you are perceived by others, seldom are you in complete control of your circumstances.

I was off to China and preparing to begin my general management journey, heading up the developing Chinese pet-care business. Exciting stuff.

Maddie and I jumped on an all-expenses-paid, four-day trip to Beijing. We were wined and dined, shown typical expat accommodation—which looked more suited to a diplomat than someone flogging dog food—and overall were made to feel very excited about a forthcoming move. But there was one small issue.

When I eventually sat down with my potential new boss, it quickly became clear that he did not like me, nor did he rate me. I certainly didn't like him. He was old school and had a reputation of 'his way or the highway'. Instantly, I was on the back foot. Most people who know me would say I'm a reasonably decent bloke with solid values. They would say that I do challenge and I do question, yet they would also say I'm respectful when doing it.

In Beijing, maybe I just got this completely wrong. Maybe I challenged too hard or gave my opinions too early, or maybe I was just crap in my interactions with him. We certainly did not connect, and under no circumstances could I work with someone I did not respect, let alone like. It hardly mattered, though, as following our friendly little meet, he was never going to sign my joining contract.

I was not in control of my agenda. Thus, I ended up leaving Mars, a company I greatly admired.

Aside

As fate would have it, I ended up joining the Wrigley Company and undertook sales and marketing director gigs before entering general management shortly after. The irony, but a brilliant one as far as I was concerned, was that in 2008, Mars Incorporated acquired Wrigley and I was immediately back in the fold. I could not have written the script better and, as I told the owners when we next met up, it only cost them $23 billion to get me back. Value for money, I said. I don't recall them smiling.

LEADING MY AGENDA

Unlike the previous story, I have two recent examples where I have instead led my agenda and executed it accordingly. On both occasions, tough up-front decisions were required.

In 2013, I was in England heading up the Wrigley business for Mars UK alongside sponsoring overall confections for Europe. I loved my time in this role. We turned the tide following years of consistent sales decline, smashed decade-long limiting beliefs, returned the business to consecutive years of growth, and were awarded the top annual financial position of all Mars segments and units worldwide. I had an infectiously driven team with exemplary values. Great people make great businesses, and the team I was part of were outstanding.

The Thomson clan were based in a beautiful little village in Berkshire, called Goring on Thames. Think posh English folk on horses, wearing customised wellington boots complete with black labs hot on their heels. It also featured the home of music icon George Michael — not my first choice in music, but that didn't stop Maddie from trying to stalk him daily at the local coffee shop!

All up, a really enjoyable time.

The problem. As with most multinationals, time in role is never a constant and already we were starting to have discussions about what would be next for us. Possibly Europe or even a stint in the United States.

In a dilemma common to many expatriates, we were at a delicate schooling age for our kids. Our eldest son, Harry, was 15 at the time and the next three years of schooling were important to us. Everyone has different perspectives on this, but for us stability in these final school years was top priority. To move again in the midst of them was a pain point that we were not willing to accept.

What ensued was a very difficult conversation with my boss, informing him of our decision to move back to Australia. When I talk about outstanding bosses who are true friends, this person was one of them. I had Ian's full support throughout the entire process, and it made a difficult decision that much easier.

Along with Ian, the business was incredibly supportive. I did an interim global role prior to running the Mars Food business back in Australia. I'd returned to Sydney and I was now a member of the global leadership team, which added new stretch and challenge.

I recount this story because this was probably the first time that I truly led my own agenda. Prior to this, my moves were largely driven by others. They were opportunistic and generally worked out very well — but I was not the one calling the shots.

I want to talk about one more moment when I have been proud of setting and controlling my own agenda.

That moment is now. Right now.

To resign after so many years at Mars was a huge decision for me. My wife and my boss both thought — and possibly still do — that I was absolutely crazy. I certainly had the 'five whys' come at me thick and fast. The only ones who seemed to get it were my old school mates — about time, you corporate nob, was their general commentary!

I may look back and question the decision, but I doubt it. As per chapter 14, the hardest part of a decision, I thought long and hard about it, made the call and there was no turning back. I needed a fresh challenge and I needed a change. Making the decision on my own terms felt bloody good.

Caveat. I do realise I am fortunate to be able to be in this position. I get it, and naturally there are times when it is that much more difficult to place yourself in the driver's seat. Fabian Dattner's critique of chapter 11, Get a life, is testament to that.

Of course, I will probably be back out there shortly when Maddie kicks me out of the house to get a real job again. When I do return to the corporate world however, I know I will be that much better. Even early immersion within the start-up and private equity world is providing new perspective and totally new thought diversity. Equally, on a personal front, being able to support Maddie's teaching career, spend quality time with the kids, do some extra studies, get some decent fitness and finally being able to commit to a weekly tennis comp has been huge. My point, however, is hopefully consistent. Do whatever you can to set and lead your own agenda. It could just be the career maker, or saver, that you're looking for.

THE PRACTICAL PART

Helping set and lead your own agenda

This framework (see figure 18.1) details three simple yet effective techniques for helping to set and own your own agenda. Don't overthink or overcomplicate, but definitely have a go at completing it.

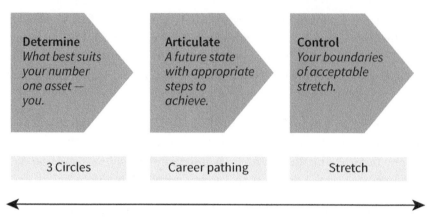

Determine
What best suits your number one asset — you.

Articulate
A future state with appropriate steps to achieve.

Control
Your boundaries of acceptable stretch.

3 Circles   Career pathing   Stretch

Models and frameworks

Figure 18.1: owning your agenda

- **Determine** your ideal company and role. One that suits you perfectly to ensure a marriage made in heaven (see figure 18.2).

- **Articulate** where you want to end up and, specifically, a path to ensure you get there (see figure 18.3, page 261).

- **Control** and set your own boundaries of acceptable stretch to a pace and path that you are comfortable with (see figure 18.4, page 262).

MODELS FOR THE WHITEBOARD

The 3 Circles

I learned this model from Nicholas Petrie. Nick was a former lead coach at the Center for Creative Leadership (CCL) in Colorado. He created this model to help re-energise careers. I think it applies at any career stage and I use it religiously to help shape, set and lead my own agenda.

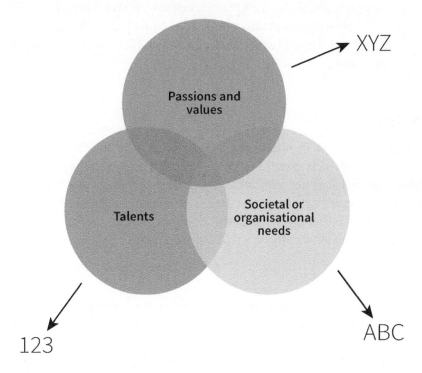

Figure 18.2: The 3 Circles

- **Circle 1: Passions and values.** Start by listing those areas that you are deeply passionate about. I also overlay my values to this list. My lead areas are purpose, autonomy and freedom, achievement, challenge and stretch, discovery and new, trust and respect, and collaboration. A long but important list for me.

- **Circle 2: Talents.** State with clarity what your actual talents are. If you are humble, this will be challenging. If not, maybe you should take some time to secure feedback from others to ensure you do not overly inflate.

- **Circle 3: Societal or organisational needs.** Essentially, this is your job. Your objective over time is to increase the size of the overlap in the middle — the one that interconnects all three circles. This means you are only working on those areas that you are passionate about and have a talent to succeed within. Success will mean you are fully aligned with the role and company that you are working for. When this happens, trust me, it's a magical feeling.

Aside

Conversely, earlier in my career, I had a brief stint in Melbourne with telecommunications giant, Ericsson. While it's a great business, it just wasn't for me. I am not a business-to-business technical type of guy, and the fit just wasn't right for both parties. Hindsight is a great thing. A good example of where I should have been setting and planning my own direction and career path with a little more advance planning.

A word of warning — please do not fool yourself by trying to match your passions with your talents or vice versa. As an example, I love writing copy for advertisements. I love it. Despite this, I know I am crap at it — my agencies and marketing directors tell me this! Equally, I used to have a talent for being very methodical and diligent in process. Nowadays, this bores me senseless and would be last on my passion list.

Career Development Framework

All good organisations will have some form of career mapping. With that said, I would be confident that 95 per cent of people, across all levels, do not have an updated long-term career plan. They will have annual development plans and hopefully genuine career conversations of substance. But unlike company strategic plans, where long-term endpoints are clearly defined and milestones are laid out like clockwork, when it comes to documenting our own personal plans, we fall woefully short.

Longer term mapping is one of the most effective ways to be in control of your own agenda.

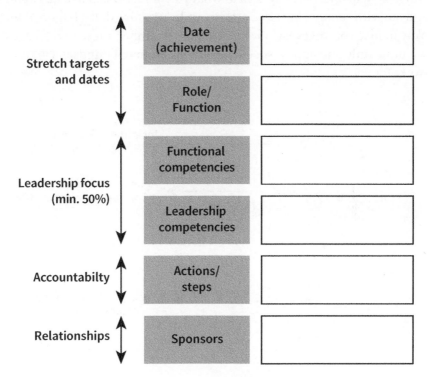

Figure 18.3: accelerated career development path

The template is a guideline only. I have developed and used it for graduates, apprentices, middle managers, directors and entry level general managers. It is not flashy, nor does it need to be. What is important is you complete and revisit it annually. I have included examples and details to complete on my website, www.hamishrthomson.com.

The Comfort Zone

This model is showcased with regularity because of its relevance. Accordingly, everyone has different views of what percentage of time we should operate within each circle. Most believe that we should never go into the panic zone. I disagree. To me, the times that you do venture there will help you discover resilience levels you never dreamed possible and will also help open your eyes as to what you are truly capable of. Dip in and out with caution, but as per Mario Andretti, know that it is more than okay to lose control every now and then! Remember, these percentages are mine only and appeal specifically to my personal mindset. Do what works for you.

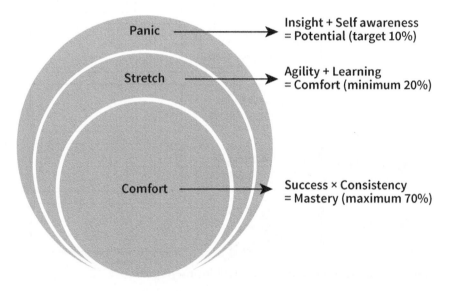

Figure 18.4: The Comfort Zone

THE CRITIQUE

A brief review from Nicholas Petrie, change expert, leadership practitioner, organisational consultant and global thought leader, Austin, Texas, USA.

....

While Hamish is clear on his preference and advice for setting your own agenda, I wonder if he is underplaying his own development over time. It appears that earlier in his career he was more content to let others set his direction and follow their lead. One reading of this is that he should have taken control earlier, that those were lost opportunities. But researchers who follow adults over the course of their lives have found that people develop through predictable stages of development.

In early adulthood most people operate from what Harvard researcher Robert Kegan calls the 'socialised mind'. Essentially, we are motivated to fit in and follow the norms and expectations of the group. This may be our peers, our company, or our tribe. It's not a bad thing, and large corporations spend a lot of time and money trying to 'socialise' their staff to follow the norms of the culture. People with this mindset are happy to follow but they don't want to lead.

Some people grow out of this stage and become 'self-authoring'. These people become the authors of their own story. They write their own script or, as Hamish says, they set their own agenda. They want to be in control, they are less concerned about what others think and they may not go along just because the company or their bosses say so. Self-authoring people make up their own mind.

Setting your own agenda is great, but it is worth acknowledging that it is a developmental achievement that only about half of adults have attained.

Researchers have found that people naturally have different levels of need for control. FIRO-B® is an assessment that looks at 'how much you want to be in control' and 'how happy are you for others to be in control of you'. Most executives score high on the former and low on the latter. They enjoy directing others but do not enjoy being directed so much.

Having worked with many executive teams over the years, I have noticed that one of the biggest causes of failure is the control levels of the leader. The worst leaders are either over controlling (read: micromanaging) or under controlling ('It's not for me to decide'). The most effective leaders can flex. Be prepared to take control but be prepared to give it away when you have competent people around you.

At the Center for Creative Leadership we found that leaders tended to grow fastest when they engaged in 'heat experiences'. These experiences have five criteria:

1. a first-time experience

2. results matter

3. chance of success or failure

4. important people are watching

5. extremely uncomfortable.

Most people try to avoid these experiences because they are so distressing. But I have seen that those people who learn to 'seek the heat' are those who do the best in their careers. Like Mario Andretti said, they are seldom in full control because they are pushing their boundaries.

I have observed that people who do this tend to move in three-year cycles. In year one they are completely over their head working out what the hell to do. In year two they are starting to deliver results. And in year three they are bored and ready to find their next heat experience. Hamish's career appears to be a good case study in this approach.

One trap I have noticed with leaders is that, although they recognise for themselves the value of heat experiences, they do the opposite to their direct reports.

Rather than giving their people difficult assignments that often cause them to struggle and sometimes fail, they will do the work themselves. At other times they will give the work to highly competent people who will find the assignment easy (and learn nothing from the experience).

They do this with good intentions ('I don't want to see my people struggle') but in doing so they 'steal heat' and development. If you want them to grow and eventually set their own agendas, let them struggle and stay close to them to help them out.

Close:
If Not You, Who?

When Sir Edmund Hillary stood at the top of Mount Everest, he looked across the valley towards the great peak Makalu and mentally worked out a route for how it could be climbed.

'It showed me that even though I was standing on top of the world, it wasn't the end of everything. I was still looking beyond to other interesting challenges.'

On top of the world, literally, and still wanting more.

Unbelievable.

'In some ways I believe I epitomise the average New Zealander: I have modest abilities, I combine these with a good deal of determination, and I rather like to succeed.'

What a legendary quote.

This is the type of leadership that inspires me.

To those who have it: never lose it.

THE CLOSE ·······································

I would have thought that the close of a book would be quite an easy thing to write. Just follow the rules of a normal business report: lead with a summary message, don't introduce anything new, sign it off with a few motivating and inspirational words of encouragement, hit the save button and move on. Foolish thought.

Now that I'm here, I have mixed views on what to say. Somewhat unnaturally, I feel indecisive. I don't like this feeling.

Let me attempt to close with hopefully two relatable learnings.

·······································

The first takes me back to Facebook HQ in London. Another poster, another strap line:

'What would you do if you weren't afraid?'

My father used to tell me that the easiest person to sell to is a salesman. This poster got me hook, line and sinker. It reminds me of the importance of always backing yourself.

I would like to think that writing this book has taken me out of my comfort zone. It has certainly tapped into a different competency set, yet at the same time it's been reassuringly familiar. Everything that I have written down has not been difficult to get out.

It's what I've experienced, where I've developed and how I've felt in the moment. When one is being truthful, it's hard to go too far wrong. Through new discovery and perspective, I know that over time some of my views and strongly held opinions will change. I like this: it indicates I'm still open to learning and growing. I hope this never changes.

I suspect I will place my crayons back in the drawer for some time. If they do venture out again, I will definitely be bolder. Watching and experiencing the idiocratic handling of the current COVID-19 pandemic has intrigued me greatly. While some global leaders have shone brightly, others have been an embarrassment and a danger to their constituents. To those who have portrayed leadership of the highest calibre, thank you. Exceptional performance not only saves lives, it provides stability, assurance and hope.

The second concept comes from a friend and former colleague. Upon telling her of my trepidations about writing this book, she replied, 'If not you, who?'

Clarity through brevity. Maybe I'll add this to the Oscar Wilde quote. Thank you, Catherine.

In closing, I hope some of my messages and learnings throughout have resonated. Ideally, even benefited.

If not you, who?

Best, Hamish

(PS — thanks Maddie and kids. ALU, APU, always)

INDEX

Printed and bound by CPI Group (UK) Ltd, Croydon, CR0 4YY

16/03/2022

03117004-0001